Seattle Mariners 2021

A Baseball Companion

Edited by Steven Goldman and Bret Sayre

Baseball Prospectus

Craig Brown, Associate Editor
Robert Au, Harry Pavlidis and Amy Pircher, Statistics Editors

Copyright © 2021 by DIY Baseball, LLC.
All rights reserved

This book or any part thereof may not be reproduced or transmitted in any form or by any means, electronic or mechanical, including photocopying, recording, or by any information storage and retrieval system, without permission in writing from the publisher.

Limit of Liability/Disclaimer of Warranty: While the publisher and the author have used their best efforts in preparing this book, they make no representations or warranties with respect to the accuracy or completeness of the contents of this book and specifically disclaim any implied warranties of merchantability or fitness for a particular purpose. No warranty may be created or extended by sales representatives or written sales materials. The advice and strategies contained herein may not be suitable for your situation. You should consult with a professional where appropriate. Neither the publisher nor the author shall be liable for any loss of profit or any other commercial damages, including but not limited to special, incidental, consequential, or other damages.

Library of Congress Cataloging-in-Publication Data:
paperback
ISBN-13: 978-1-950716-73-9

Project Credits
Cover Design: Ginny Searle
Interior Design and Production: Amy Pircher, Robert Au
Layout: Amy Pircher, Robert Au

Baseball icon courtesy of Uberux, from https://www.shareicon.net/author/uberux

Ballpark diagram courtesy of Lou Spirito/THIRTY81 Project, https://thirty81project.com/

Manufactured in the United States of America
10 9 8 7 6 5 4 3 2 1

Table of Contents

Statistical Introduction v

Part 1: Team Analysis
Performance Graphs 3
2020 Team Performance 4
2021 Team Projections 5
Team Personnel 6
T-Mobile Park Stats 7
Mariners Team Analysis 9

Part 2: Player Analysis
Mariners Player Analysis 16
Mariners Prospects 89

Part 3: Featured Articles
Mariners All-Time Top 10 Players 101
    by Patrick Dubuque

A Taxonomy of 2020 Abnormalities 109
    by Rob Mains

Tranches of WAR 115
    by Russell A. Carleton

Secondhand Sport 121
    by Patrick Dubuque

Steve Dalkowski Dreaming 125
    by Steven Goldman

A Reward For A Functioning Society 129
    by Cory Frontin and Craig Goldstein

Index of Names 133

Statistical Introduction

Sports are, fundamentally, a blend of athletic endeavor and storytelling. Baseball, like any other sport, tells its stories in so many ways: in the arc of a game from the stands or a season from the box scores, in photos, or even in numbers. At Baseball Prospectus, we understand that statistics don't replace observation or any of baseball's stories, but complement everything else that makes the game so much fun.

What stats help us with is with patterns and precision, variance and value. This book can help you learn things you may not see from watching a game or hundred, whether it's the path of a career over time or the breadth of the entire MLB. We'd also never ask you to choose between our numbers and the experience of viewing a game from the cheap seats or the comfort of your home; our publication combines running the numbers with observations and wisdom from some of the brightest minds we can find. But if you *do* want to learn more about the numbers beyond what's on the backs of player jerseys, let us help explain.

Offense

We've revised our methodology for determining batting value. Long-time readers of the book will notice that we've retired True Average in favor of a new metric: Deserved Runs Created Plus (DRC+). Developed by Jonathan Judge and our stats team, this statistic measures everything a player does at the plate–reaching base, hitting for power, making outs, and moving runners over–and puts it on a scale where 100 equals league-average performance. A DRC+ of 150 is terrific, a DRC+ of 100 is average and a DRC+ of 75 means you better be an excellent defender.

DRC+ also does a better job than any of our previous metrics in taking contextual factors into account. The model adjusts for how the park affects performance, but also for things like the talent of the opposing pitcher, value of different types of batted-ball events, league, temperature and other factors. It's able to describe a player's expected offensive contribution than any other statistic we've found over the years, and also does a better job of predicting future performance as well.

The other aspect of run-scoring is baserunning, which we quantify using Baserunning Runs. BRR not only records the value of stolen bases (or getting caught in the act), but also accounts for all the stuff that doesn't show up on the back of a baseball card: a runner's ability to go first to third on a single, or advance on a fly ball.

Defense

Where offensive value is *relatively* easy to identify and understand, defensive value is ... not. Over the past dozen years, the sabermetric community has focused mostly on stats based on zone data: a real-live human person records the type of batted ball and estimated landing location, and models are created that give expected outs. From there, you can compare fielders' actual outs to those expected ones. Simple, right?

Unfortunately, zone data has two major issues. First, zone data is recorded by commercial data providers who keep the raw data private unless you pay for it. (All the statistics we build in this book and on our website use public data as inputs.) That hurts our ability to test assumptions or duplicate results. Second, over the years it has become apparent that there's quite a bit of "noise" in zone-based fielding analysis. Sometimes the conclusions drawn from zone data don't hold up to scrutiny, and sometimes the different data provided by different providers don't look anything alike, giving wildly different results. Sometimes the hard-working professional stringers or scorers might unknowingly inflict unconscious bias into the mix: for example good fielders will often be credited with more expected outs despite the data, and ballparks with high press boxes tend to score more line drives than ones with a lower press box.

Enter our Fielding Runs Above Average (FRAA). For most positions, FRAA is built from play-by-play data, which allows us to avoid the subjectivity found in many other fielding metrics. The idea is this: count how many fielding plays are made by a given player and compare that to expected plays for an average fielder at their position (based on pitcher ground ball tendencies and batter handedness). Then we adjust for park and base-out situations.

When it comes to catchers, our methodology is a little different thanks to the laundry list of responsibilities they're tasked with beyond just, well, catching and throwing the ball. By now you've probably heard about "framing" or the art of making umpires more likely to call balls outside the strike zone for strikes. To put this into one tidy number, we incorporate pitch tracking data (for the years it exists) and adjust for important factors like pitcher, umpire, batter and home-field advantage using a mixed-model approach. This grants us a number for how many strikes the catcher is personally adding to (or subtracting from) his pitchers' performance ... which we then convert to runs added or lost using linear weights.

Framing is one of the biggest parts of determining catcher value, but we also take into account blocking balls from going past, whether a scorer deems it a passed ball or a wild pitch. We use a similar approach—one that really benefits from the pitch tracking data that tells us what ends up in the dirt and what doesn't. We also include a catcher's ability to prevent stolen bases and how well they field balls in play, and *finally* we come up with our FRAA for catchers.

Pitching

Both pitching and fielding make up the half of baseball that isn't run scoring: run prevention. Separating pitching from fielding is a tough task, and most recent pitching analysis has branched off from Voros McCracken's famous (and controversial) statement, "There is little if any difference among major-league pitchers in their ability to prevent hits on balls hit in the field of play." The research of the analytic community has validated this to some extent, and there are a host of "defense-independent" pitching measures that have been developed to try and extract the effect of the defense behind a hurler from the pitcher's work.

Our solution to this quandary is Deserved Run Average (DRA), our core pitching metric. DRA seeks to evaluate a pitcher's performance, much like earned run average (ERA), the tried-and-true pitching stat you've seen on every baseball broadcast or box score from the past century, but it's very different. To start, DRA takes an event-by-event look at what the pitchers does, and adjusts the value of that event based on different environmental factors like park, batter, catcher, umpire, base-out situation, run differential, inning, defense, home field advantage, pitcher role and temperature. That mixed model gives us a pitcher's expected contribution, similar to what we do for our DRC+ model for hitters and FRAA model for catchers. (Oh, and we also consider the pitcher's effect on basestealing and on balls getting past the catcher.)

DRA is set to the scale of runs allowed per nine innings (RA9) instead of ERA, which makes DRA's scale slightly higher than ERA's. Because of this, for ease of use, we're supplying DRA-, which is much easier for the reader to parse. As with DRC+, DRA- is an "index" stat, meaning instead of using some arbitrary and shifting number to denote what's "good," average is always 100. The reason that it uses a minus rather than a plus is because like ERA, a lower number is better. Therefore a 75 DRA- describes a performance 25 percent better than average, whereas a 150 DRA- means that either a pitcher is getting extremely lucky with their results, or getting ready to try a new pitch.

Since the last time you picked up an edition of this book, we've also made a few minor changes to DRA to make it better. Recent research into "tunneling"—the act of throwing consecutive pitches that appear similar from a batter's point of view until after the swing decision point–data has given us a new contextual factor to account for in DRA: plate distance. This refers to the

Seattle Mariners 2021

distance between successive pitches as they approach the plate, and while it has a smaller effect than factors like velocity or whiff rate, it still can help explain pitcher strikeout rate in our model.

Recently Added Descriptive Statistics

Returning to our 2021 edition of the book are a few figures which recently appeared. These numbers may be a little bit more familiar to those of you who have spent some time investigating baseball statistics.

Fastball Percentage

Our fastball percentage (FA%) statistic measures how frequently a pitcher throws a pitch classified as a "fastball," measured as a percentage of overall pitches thrown. We qualify three types of fastballs:

1. The traditional four-seam fastball;
2. The two-seam fastball or sinker;
3. "Hard cutters," which are pitches that have the movement profile of a cut fastball and are used as the pitcher's primary offering or in place of a more traditional fastball.

For example, a pitcher with a FA% of 67 throws any combination of these three pitches about two-thirds of the time.

Whiff Rate

Everybody loves a swing and a miss, and whiff rate (Whiff%) measures how frequently pitchers induce a swinging strike. To calculate Whiff%, we add up all the pitches thrown that ended with a swinging strike, then divide that number by a pitcher's total pitches thrown. Most often, high whiff rates correlate with high strikeout rates (and overall effective pitcher performance).

Called Strike Probability

Called Strike Probability (CSP) is a number that represents the likelihood that all of a pitcher's pitches will be called a strike while controlling for location, pitcher and batter handedness, umpire and count. Here's how it works: on each pitch, our model determines how many times (out of 100) that a similar pitch was called for a strike given those factors mentioned above, and when normalized for each batter's strike zone. Then we average the CSP for all pitches thrown by a pitcher in a season, and that gives us the yearly CSP percentage you see in the stats boxes.

As you might imagine, pitchers with a higher CSP are more likely to work in the zone, where pitchers with a lower CSP are likely locating their pitches outside the normal strike zone, for better or for worse.

Projections

Many of you aren't turning to this book just for a look at what a player has done, but for a look at what a player is going to do: the PECOTA projections. PECOTA, initially developed by Nate Silver (who has moved on to greater fame as a political analyst), consists of three parts:

1. Major-league equivalencies, which use minor-league statistics to project how a player will perform in the major leagues;
2. Baseline forecasts, which use weighted averages and regression to the mean to estimate a player's current true talent level; and
3. Aging curves, which uses the career paths of comparable players to estimate how a player's statistics are likely to change over time.

With all those important things covered, let's take a look at what's in the book this year.

Team Prospectus

Most of this book is composed of team chapters, with one for each of the 30 major-league franchises. On the first page of each chapter, you'll see a box that contains some of the key statistics for each team as well as a very inviting stadium diagram.

We start with the team name, their unadjusted 2020 win-loss record, and their divisional ranking. Beneath that are a host of other team statistics. **Pythag** presents an adjusted 2020 winning percentage, calculated by taking runs scored per game (**RS/G**) and runs allowed per game (**RA/G**) for the team, and running them through a version of Bill James' Pythagorean formula that was refined and improved by David Smyth and Brandon Heipp. (The formula is called "Pythagenpat," which is equally fun to type and to say.)

Next up is **DRC+**, described earlier, to indicate the overall hitting ability of the team either above or below league-average. Run prevention on the pitching side is covered by **DRA** (also mentioned earlier) and another metric: Fielding Independent Pitching (**FIP**), which calculates another ERA-like statistic based on strikeouts, walks, and home runs recorded. Defensive Efficiency Rating (**DER**) tells us the percentage of balls in play turned into outs for the team, and is a quick fielding shorthand that rounds out run prevention.

After that, we have several measures related to roster composition, as opposed to on-field performance. **B-Age** and **P-Age** tell us the average age of a team's batters and pitchers, respectively. **Payroll** is the combined team payroll for all on-field players, and Doug Pappas' Marginal Dollars per Marginal Win (**M$/MW**) tells us how much money a team spent to earn production above replacement level.

Next to each of these stats, we've listed each team's MLB rank in that category from first to 30th. In this, first always indicates a positive outcome and 30th a negative outcome, except in the case of salary—first is highest.

After the franchise statistics, we share a few items about the team's home ballpark. There's the aforementioned diagram of the park's dimensions (including distances to the outfield wall), a graphic showing the height of the wall from the left-field pole to the right-field pole, and a table showing three-year park factors for the stadium. The park factors are displayed as indexes where 100 is average, 110 means that the park inflates the statistic in question by 10 percent, and 90 means that the park deflates the statistic in question by 10 percent.

On the second page of each team chapter, you'll find three graphs. The first is **Payroll History** and helps you see how the team's payroll has compared to the MLB and divisional average payrolls over time. Payroll figures are current as of January 1, 2021; with so many free agents still unsigned as of this writing, the final 2021 figure will likely be significantly different for many teams. (In the meantime, you can always find the most current data at Baseball Prospectus' Cot's Baseball Contracts page.)

The second graph is **Future Commitments** and helps you see the team's future outlays, if any.

The third graph is **Farm System Ranking** and displays how the Baseball Prospectus prospect team has ranked the organization's farm system since 2007.

After the graphs, we have a **Personnel** section that lists many of the important decision-makers and upper-level field and operations staff members for the franchise, as well as any former Baseball Prospectus staff members who are currently part of the organization. (In very rare circumstances, someone might be on both lists!)

Position Players

After all that information and a thoughtful bylined essay covering each team, we present our player comments. These are also bylined, but due to frequent franchise shifts during the offseason, our bylines are more a rough guide than a perfect accounting of who wrote what.

Each player is listed with the major-league team that employed him as of early January 2021. If a player changed teams after that point via free agency, trade, or any other method, you'll be able to find them in the chapter for their previous squad.

As an example, take a look at the player comment for Padres shortstop Fernando Tatis Jr.: the stat block that accompanies his written comment is at the top of this page. First we cover biographical information (age is as of June 30, 2021) before moving onto the stats themselves. Our statistic columns include standard identifying information like **YEAR**, **TEAM**, **LVL** (level of affiliated play) and **AGE** before getting into the numbers. Next, we provide raw, untranslated

Fernando Tatis Jr. SS

Born: 01/02/99   Age: 22   Bats: R   Throws: R
Height: 6'3"   Weight: 217   Origin: International Free Agent, 2015

YEAR	TEAM	LVL	AGE	PA	R	2B	3B	HR	RBI	BB	K	SB	CS	AVG/OBP/SLG
2018	SA	AA	19	394	77	22	4	16	43	33	109	16	5	.286/.355/.507
2019	SD	MLB	20	372	61	13	6	22	53	30	110	16	6	.317/.379/.590
2020	SD	MLB	21	257	50	11	2	17	45	27	61	11	3	.277/.366/.571
2021 FS	SD	MLB	22	600	95	24	4	31	81	50	165	17	8	.263/.331/.499
2021 DC	SD	MLB	22	628	100	25	4	32	85	53	173	19	8	.263/.331/.499

Comparables: Darryl Strawberry, Bo Bichette, Ronald Acuña Jr.

YEAR	TEAM	LVL	AGE	PA	DRC+	BABIP	BRR	FRAA	WARP
2018	SA	AA	19	394	136	.370	3.0	SS(83): -1.9	2.4
2019	SD	MLB	20	372	118	.410	7.1	SS(83): 0.9	3.4
2020	SD	MLB	21	257	126	.306	0.7	SS(57): -5.5	0.9
2021 FS	SD	MLB	22	600	126	.318	1.7	SS -1	3.9
2021 DC	SD	MLB	22	628	126	.318	1.8	SS -1	4.0

numbers like you might find on the back of your dad's baseball cards: **PA** (plate appearances), **R** (runs), **2B** (doubles), **3B** (triples), **HR** (home runs), **RBI** (runs batted in), **BB** (walks), **K** (strikeouts), **SB** (stolen bases) and **CS** (caught stealing).

Following the basic stats is **Whiff%** (whiff rate), which denotes how often, when a batter swings, he fails to make contact with the ball. Another way to think of this number is an inverse of a hitter's contact rate.

Next, we have unadjusted "slash" statistics: **AVG** (batting average), **OBP** (on-base percentage) and **SLG** (slugging percentage). Following the slash line is **DRC+** (Deserved Runs Created Plus), which we described earlier as total offensive expected contribution compared to the league average.

BABIP (batting average on balls in play) tells us how often a ball in play fell for a hit, and can help us identify whether a batter may have been lucky or not ... but note that high BABIPs also tend to follow the great hitters of our time, as well as speedy singles hitters who put the ball on the ground.

The next item is **BRR** (Baserunning Runs), which covers all of a player's baserunning accomplishments including (but not limited to) swiped bags and failed attempts. Next is **FRAA** (Fielding Runs Above Average), which also includes the number of games previously played at each position noted in parentheses. Multi-position players have only their two most frequent positions listed here, but their total FRAA number reflects all positions played.

Our last column here is **WARP** (Wins Above Replacement Player). WARP estimates the total value of a player, which means for hitters it takes into account hitting runs above average (calculated using the DRC+ model), BRR and FRAA. Then, it makes an adjustment for positions played and gives the player a credit for plate appearances based upon the difference between "replacement level"—which is derived from the quality of players added to a team's roster after the start of the season–and the league average.

The final line just below the stats box is **PECOTA** data, which is discussed further in a following section.

Catchers

Catchers are a special breed, and thus they have earned their own separate box which displays some of the defensive metrics that we've built just for them. As an example, let's check out Yasmani Grandal.

YEAR	TEAM	P. COUNT	FRM RUNS	BLK RUNS	THRW RUNS	TOT RUNS
2018	LAD	16816	15.7	0.8	0.1	16.5
2019	MIL	18740	19.4	1.8	-0.1	21.1
2020	CHW	4830	3.7	0.3	-0.2	3.8
2021	CHW	14430	16.7	-0.6	1.0	17.1
2021	CHW	14430	16.7	0.4	1.0	18.0

The **YEAR** and **TEAM** columns match what you'd find in the other stat box. **P. COUNT** indicates the number of pitches thrown while the catcher was behind the plate, including swinging strikes, fouls and balls in play. **FRM RUNS** is the total run value the catcher provided (or cost) his team by influencing the umpire to call strikes where other catchers did not. **BLK RUNS** expresses the total run value above or below average for the catcher's ability to prevent wild pitches and passed balls. **THRW RUNS** is calculated using a similar model as the previous two statistics, and it measures a catcher's ability to throw out basestealers but also to dissuade them from testing his arm in the first place. It takes into account factors like the pitcher (including his delivery and pickoff move) and baserunner (who could be as fast as Billy Hamilton or as slow as Yonder Alonso). **TOT RUNS** is the sum of all of the previous three statistics.

Pitchers

Let's give our pitchers a turn, using 2020 AL Cy Young winner Shane Bieber as our example. Take a look at his stat block: the first line and the **YEAR**, **TEAM**, **LVL** and **AGE** columns are the same as in the position player example earlier.

Here too, we have a series of columns that display raw, unadjusted statistics compiled by the pitcher over the course of a season: **W** (wins), **L** (losses), **SV** (saves), **G** (games pitched), **GS** (games started), **IP** (innings pitched), **H** (hits allowed) and **HR** (home runs allowed). Next we have two statistics that are rates: **BB/9** (walks per nine innings) and **K/9** (strikeouts per nine innings), before returning to the unadjusted K (strikeouts).

Next up is **GB%** (ground ball percentage), which is the percentage of all batted balls that were hit on the ground, including both outs and hits. Remember, this is based on observational data and subject to human error, so please approach this with a healthy dose of skepticism.

BABIP (batting average on balls in play) is calculated using the same methodology as it is for position players, but it often tells us more about a pitcher than it does a hitter. With pitchers, a high BABIP is often due to poor defense or bad luck, and can often be an indicator of potential rebound, and a low BABIP may be cause to expect performance regression. (A typical league-average BABIP is close to .290–.300.)

The metrics **WHIP** (walks plus hits per inning pitched) and **ERA** (earned run average) are old standbys: WHIP measures walks and hits allowed on a per-inning basis, while ERA measures earned runs on a nine-inning basis. Neither of these stats are translated or adjusted.

DRA- (Deserved Run Average) was described at length earlier, and measures how the pitcher "deserved" to perform compared to other pitchers. Please note that since we lack all the data points that would make for a "real" DRA for minor-league events, the DRA- displayed for minor league partial-seasons is based off of different data. (That data is a modified version of our cFIP metric, which you can find more information about on our website.)

Shane Bieber   RHP

Born: 05/31/95   Age: 26   Bats: R   Throws: R
Height: 6'3"   Weight: 200   Origin: Round 4, 2016 Draft (#122 overall)

YEAR	TEAM	LVL	AGE	W	L	SV	G	GS	IP	H	HR	BB/9	K/9	K	GB%	BABIP
2018	AKR	AA	23	3	0	0	5	5	31	26	1	0.3	8.7	30	47.3%	.278
2018	COL	AAA	23	3	1	0	8	8	48^2	30	3	1.1	8.7	47	52.0%	.227
2018	CLE	MLB	23	11	5	0	20	19	114^2	130	13	1.8	9.3	118	46.2%	.356
2019	CLE	MLB	24	15	8	0	34	33	214^1	186	31	1.7	10.9	259	44.4%	.298
2020	CLE	MLB	25	8	1	0	12	12	77^1	46	7	2.4	14.2	122	48.4%	.267
2021 FS	CLE	MLB	26	10	6	0	26	26	150	121	18	2.1	11.7	195	45.5%	.297
2021 DC	CLE	MLB	26	14	7	0	30	30	196.7	159	24	2.1	11.7	257	45.5%	.297

Comparables: Luis Severino, Danny Salazar, Joe Musgrove

YEAR	TEAM	LVL	AGE	WHIP	ERA	DRA-	WARP	MPH	FB%	WHF	CSP
2018	AKR	AA	23	0.87	1.16	61	0.9				
2018	COL	AAA	23	0.74	1.66	69	1.2				
2018	CLE	MLB	23	1.33	4.55	74	2.6	94.7	57.4%	26.2%	
2019	CLE	MLB	24	1.05	3.28	75	4.9	94.4	45.8%	30.8%	
2020	CLE	MLB	25	0.87	1.63	53	2.6	95.3	53.6%	40.7%	
2021 FS	CLE	MLB	26	1.04	2.44	64	4.4	94.7	50.0%	33.2%	44.2%
2021 DC	CLE	MLB	26	1.04	2.44	64	5.8	94.7	50.0%	33.2%	44.2%

Just like with hitters, **WARP** (Wins Above Replacement Player) is a total value metric that puts pitchers of all stripes on the same scale as position players. We use DRA as the primary input for our calculation of WARP. You might notice that relief pitchers (due to their limited innings) may have a lower WARP than you were expecting or than you might see in other WARP-like metrics. WARP does not take leverage into account, just the actions a pitcher performs and the expected value of those actions … which ends up judging high-leverage relief pitchers differently than you might imagine given their prestige and market value.

MPH gives you the pitcher's 95th percentile velocity for the noted season, in order to give you an idea of what the *peak* fastball velocity a pitcher possesses. Since this comes from our pitch-tracking data, it is not publicly available for minor-league pitchers.

Finally, we display the three new pitching metrics we described earlier. **FB%** (fastball percentage) gives you the percentage of fastballs thrown out of all pitches. **WHF** (whiff rate) tells you the percentage of swinging strikes induced out of all pitches. **CSP** (called strike probability) expresses the likelihood of all pitches thrown to result in a called strike, after controlling for factors like handedness, umpire, pitch type, count and location.

PECOTA

All players have PECOTA projections for 2021, as well as a set of other numbers that describe the performance of comparable players according to PECOTA. All projections for 2021 are for the player at the date we went to press in early January and are projected into the league and park context as indicated by the team abbreviation. (Note that players at very low levels of the minors are too unpredictable to assess using these numbers.) All PECOTA projected statistics represent a player's projected major-league performance.

How we're doing that is a little different this season. There are really two different values that go into the final stat line that you see for PECOTA: How a player performs, and how much playing time he'll be given to perform it. In the past we've estimated playing time based on each team's roster and depth charts, and we'll continue to do that. These projections are denoted as **2021 DC**.

But in many cases, a player won't be projected for major-league playing time; most of the time this is because they aren't projected to be major-league players at all, but still developing as prospects. Or perhaps a player will provide Triple-A depth, only to have an opportunity open up because of injury. For these purposes, we're also supplying a second projection, labeled **2021 FS**, or full season. This is what we would project the player to provide in 600 plate appearances or 150 innings pitched.

Below the projections are the player's three highest-scoring comparable players as determined by PECOTA. All comparables represent a snapshot of how the listed player was performing at the same age as the current player, so if a

23-year-old pitcher is compared to Bartolo Colón, he's actually being compared to a 23-year-old Colón, not the version that pitched for the Rangers in 2018, nor to Colón's career as a whole.

A few points about pitcher projections. First, we aren't yet projecting peak velocity, so that column will be blank in the PECOTA lines. Second, projecting DRA is trickier than evaluating past performance, because it is unclear how deserving each pitcher will be of his anticipated outcomes. However, we know that another DRA-related statistic–contextual FIP or cFIP-estimates future run scoring very well. So for PECOTA, the projected DRA- figures you see are based on the past cFIPs generated by the pitcher and comparable players over time, along with the other factors described above.

If you're familiar with PECOTA, then you'll have noticed that the projection system often appears bullish on players coming off a bad year and bearish on players coming off a good year. (This is because the system weights several previous seasons, not just the most recent one.) In addition, we publish the 50th percentile projections for each player–which is smack in the middle of the range of projected production—which tends to mean PECOTA stat lines don't often have extreme results like 40 home runs or 250 strikeouts in a given season. In essence, PECOTA doesn't project very many extreme seasons.

Managers

After all those wonderful team chapters, we've got statistics for each big-league manager, all of whom are organized by alphabetical order. Here you'll find a block including an extraordinary amount of information collected from each manager's entire career. For more information on the acronyms and what they mean, please visit the Glossary at www.baseballprospectus.com.

There is one important metric that we'd like to call attention to, and you'll find it next to each manager's name: **wRM+** (weighted reliever management plus). Developed by Rob Arthur and Rian Watt, wRM+ investigates how good a manager is at using their best relievers during the moments of highest leverage, using both our proprietary DRA metric as well as Leverage Index. wRM+ is scaled to a league average of 100, and a wRM+ of 105 indicates that relievers were used approximately five percent "better" than average. On the other hand, a wRM+ of 95 would tell us the team used its relievers five percent "worse" than the average team.

While wRM+ does not have an extremely strong correlation with a manager, it is statistically significant; this means that a manager is not *entirely* responsible for a team's wRM+, but does have some effect on that number.

Part 1: Team Analysis

Performance Graphs

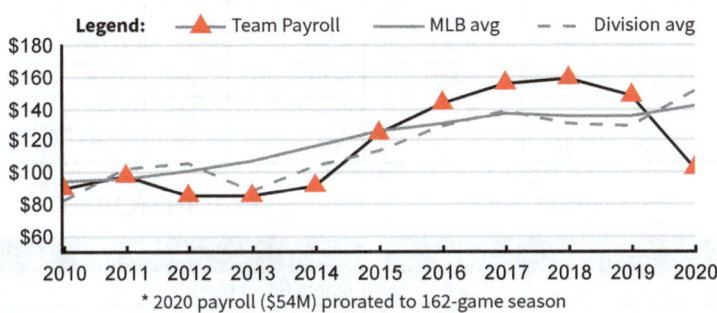

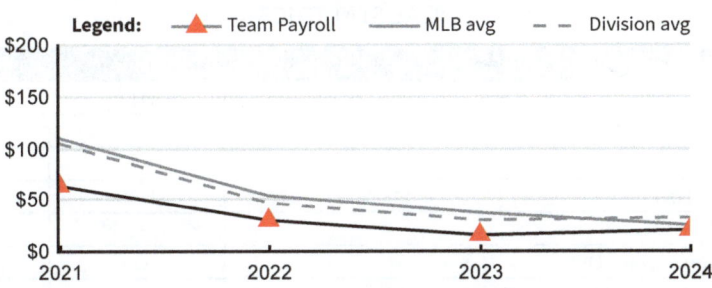

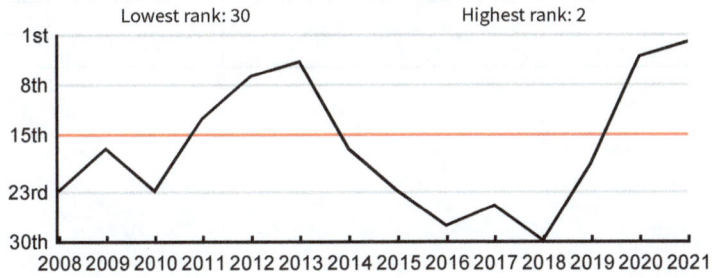

2020 Team Performance

ACTUAL STANDINGS

Team	W	L	Pct
OAK	36	24	0.600
HOU	29	31	0.483
SEA	**27**	**33**	**0.450**
LAA	26	34	0.433
TEX	22	38	0.367

dWIN% STANDINGS

Team	W	L	Pct
OAK	29	31	0.499
LAA	29	31	0.497
HOU	28	32	0.472
SEA	**22**	**38**	**0.370**
TEX	18	42	0.304

TOP HITTERS

Player	WARP
Kyle Seager	1.8
J.P. Crawford	1.2
Kyle Lewis	1.0

TOP PITCHERS

Player	WARP
Marco Gonzales	1.0
Yusei Kikuchi	0.8
Justus Sheffield	0.8

VITAL STATISTICS

Statistic Name	Value	Rank
Pythagenpat	.417	25th
dWin%	.370	27th
Runs Scored per Game	4.23	23rd
Runs Allowed per Game	5.05	21st
Deserved Runs Created Plus	93	24th
Deserved Run Average Minus	114	27th
Fielding Independent Pitching	5.00	24th
Defensive Efficiency Rating	.712	4th
Batter Age	27.2	6th
Pitcher Age	26.9	1st
Payroll	$54.0M	18th
Marginal $ per Marginal Win	$4.0M	17th

2021 Team Projections

PROJECTED STANDINGS

Team	W	L	Pct	+/-
HOU	92.5	69.5	0.571	14
There's reason to be skeptical of the starting pitching depth, but this team will score plenty of runs.				
LAA	86.2	75.8	0.532	16
Still buying pitching from the bargain bin despite a new GM, they lack the depth to be great, but if the stars stay healthy, they'll be good.				
OAK	82.2	79.8	0.507	-15
Free-agent departures in the outfield, infield, and bullpen leave them scrambling for coverage despite Matts Chapman and Olson.				
SEA	**70.7**	**91.3**	**0.436**	**-2**
The rebuild should be nearly over, but will go on for at least another year after a shockingly silent winter.				
TEX	66.8	95.2	0.412	7
A team in total, chaotic transition, but the kids could be fun to watch.				

TOP PROJECTED HITTERS

Player	WARP
Mitch Haniger	2.3
J.P. Crawford	2.0
Kyle Lewis	1.9

TOP PROJECTED PITCHERS

Player	WARP
James Paxton	2.0
Marco Gonzales	1.9
Yusei Kikuchi	1.3

FARM SYSTEM REPORT

Top Prospect	Number of Top 101 Prospects
Julio Y. Rodriguez	6

KEY DEDUCTIONS

Player	WARP

KEY ADDITIONS

Player	WARP
Rafael Montero	0.7
Chris Flexen	0.6

Team Personnel

Executive Vice President and General Manager
Jerry Dipoto

Vice President & Assistant General Manager
Justin Hollander

Senior Director, Analytics
Jess Smith

Director, Player Development
Andy McKay

Director, Amateur Scouting
Scott Hunter

Manager
Scott Servais

BP Alumni
John Choiniere

T-Mobile Park Stats

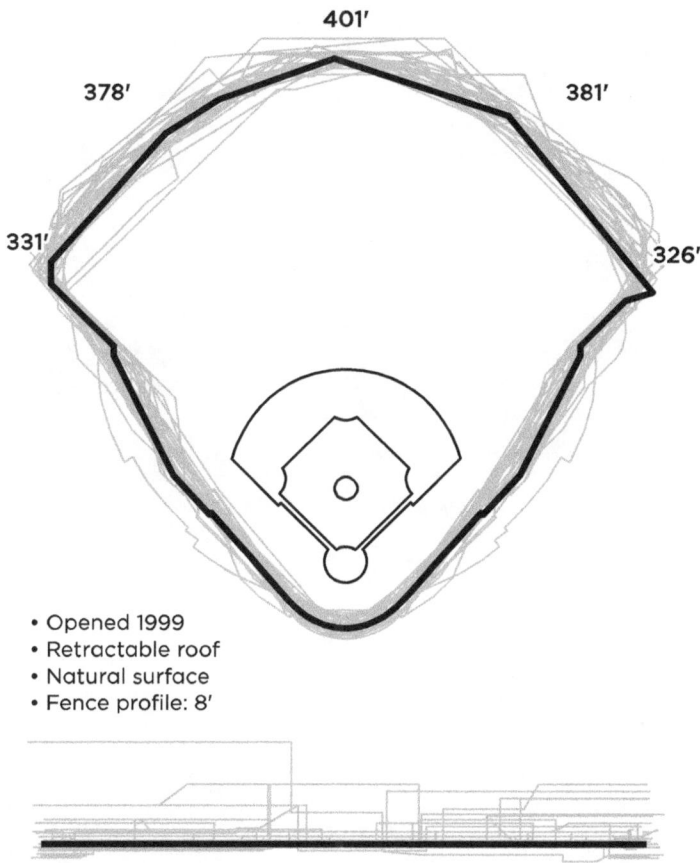

- Opened 1999
- Retractable roof
- Natural surface
- Fence profile: 8'

Three-Year Park Factors

Runs	Runs/RH	Runs/LH	HR/RH	HR/LH
96	97	95	99	95

Mariners Team Analysis

The 20th anniversary of the Kingdome's implosion—March 26, 2000—shouldn't have been a news item in 2020. It was Opening Day of Major League Baseball! But then, on March 9, Rudy Gobert caressed some microphones, and North American professional sports fell like so many dominos, with MLB spring training pressing pause on the ominous date of Friday the 13th. On that day, Commissioner Manfred said the regular season would be postponed for at least two weeks—but everyone knew it would be much longer than that.

Sports stations were suddenly desperate for content. On TV, they replayed entire postseasons, while websites featured athletes' at-home workout regimens (remember the dog squats, those patient retrievers and black labs?) and deep-fried turkey tips (care of the Mariners' own Marco Gonzales). After talking through possible rosters upwards and down, hosts reached out to every sort of adjacent content (including debut novelists who reimagined the 2011 spring training to include a fictional team called the LA Lions, ahem). There were a lot of highlight reels.

March 26 arrived: Opening Day, except not. Cue the dynamite. Watching that gray henge crumble in 2020 felt one part nostalgic, one part portent for the season ahead—a dramatic explosion, expectations (and edifices) go poof, and then we're left with nothing but this lurking cloud of particulate. The detonation of 2020 was unplanned, of course, but in 2000 the implosion was very much engineered—a feat, even. In a span shorter than the time it takes to sing "Take me Out to the Ball Game," over 20 miles of detonation cord, wicked along the ribs of the dome and around its concrete body, went off in a coordinated ignition that looked downright orchestral. As one newscaster said at the time, it was an "unbelievable sight to see a completely functional building turned to dust in fifteen seconds." Well, mostly functional. It did have a bad habit of dropping ceiling tiles, and architecture critic Paul Goldberger wrote that the multi-purpose concrete dome was cursed with "a deadly heavy-handedness."

That March 2000 day in Seattle was a memorable one. Elliott Bay was full of bobbing sailboats—the Kingdome sat just a few blocks away from the water—and Seattlites perched on hills and overpasses around the city. The explosions started, the building went down, cheers went up on hills. Seattle had already fallen in love with its new Safeco Field; to the Kingdome they said good riddance.

Seattle Mariners 2021

It's worth focusing on those hills for a second: Lore is that Seattle has seven hills, just like Rome, but the fact well known to any biker or driver of a manual transmission is that the city has plenty more than that. It's just that this town, younger than baseball, in a state itself established a dozen years after the National League, still has a chip on its shoulder about its relative youth, and august associations could only help with credibility. Right?

While Seattle may be one of the league's younger teams (it and the Blue Jays joined the majors in 1977), they are the only active team left to not have appeared in the World Series. If postseason performance is a sign of a club's maturity, if reaching the Fall Classic some sort of arrival into adulthood and legitimacy, then the team's lack of arrival is keeping it what—eternally young? That the Mariners hold another ignoble title again as they enter into the 2021 season—the longest current drought of postseason appearances among the four major American sports—signals either immaturity or obsolescence. To look at the Mariners' lineup (with Dee Gordon's departure, at the time of this writing, only one player on the 40-man roster, third baseman Kyle Seager, was born before 1990), it is certainly the former. In 2020 the Mariners had the youngest team in the league, and while it'll be a few months until we can determine if they'll hold that distinction again in 2021, even the addition of a few veterans can't bring their average up by much.

Youth can be a hindrance to success, a handicap or inferiority complex, but it is important to Seattle's identity, too. The Mariners have made a franchise of catching athletes at the start of their careers. On his first pitch, April 10, 1989, Ken Griffey Jr. hit a home run. He was still (barely) a teenager at the time of the blast, but he earned the moniker "The Kid" and kept it well into his 20s and along his course to becoming a generational player. Alex Rodriguez was drafted by the Mariners at 17, had his own set of teenage plate appearances, and spent his less-complicated early 20s with the Mariners, four of those years as an All-Star. Randy Johnson may have gone into the Hall of Fame as a Diamondback (a decision that still stings to many Seattleites), but first, he struck out over 2,000 batters as a Mariner.

Off the field, a few generations of youth culture (Jimi Hendrix, Nirvana) helped keep Seattle young in the eyes of the nation's cultural zeitgeist. Lest you forget, Nirvana's "Smells like Teen Spirit," that anthem of disaffected adolescence, came out of Seattle, and for a reason. That Seattle was new but not so new, self-aware but not self-empowered, could describe the city and its baseball team. When you reach the kind of wall a surly adolescence presents, there are two options: slouch against it or climb over it. More seasons than not, Seattle's tried for number two, couldn't gain purchase, and settled for option one.

Along with that slouching posture, Seattle has a habit of helping itself along in the chutes-and-ladders game of starting back at zero, of forever preserving its youth (even when it doesn't intend to). The Great Seattle Fire, for one: that wiped out its oldest neighborhood. That implosion was unintended, while other destructions felt more mindful: in the early twentieth century Seattle made a practice of cutting into those vista-ful hills and regrading them so their slopes could become viable real estate. A byproduct was that the tidal flats just south of downtown got a lot of new dirt. That dirt became a neighborhood (Sodo) and its warehouse and industrial uses slowly got pushed aside to make way for Seattle's sports franchises and their parking lots (enter the Kingdome).

The Mariners have had their own series of implosive moments, some intentional demolitions, some less so. Griffey's busted wrist, incurred in a collision with the centerfield wall: unintentional. Lou Pinella's tirades: intentional. Loyal fans will remember the 2008 Mariners being the first team to reach the shameful milestone of 100-losses with a $100-million payroll. Cue the dynamite in the front office. The implosion of the next GM, Jack Zduriencik, was more of a slow-motion collapse, also not intended. Jerry Dipoto followed, and the current GM managed to implode his first plan (which involved decimating the farm system in search of the wild-card berth) and still keep his job. On to plan two, which involves building up the youngest team in baseball so it becomes a viable contender in the early part of the 2020s.

Dipoto predicted the 2019 season would not be objectively good (and, at 68-94, it was not); the 2020 season was one he thought held promise. As discussed in last year's Baseball Prospectus, he predicted by 2020 or 2021, the Mariners would be "a threat to win the World Series." That obviously didn't happen in 2020. The Mariners, in their shortened season, landed with a respectably bad 27-33—better than many in the majors, but still not within reach of the expanded playoff bracket. Many an M's fan felt a little flutter of hope in Marco Gonzales complete game against the Angels, wherein he struck out Mike Trout three times. Trout's bad game might not have been a proper implosion, but it was a pretty satisfying wipeout.

Dipoto was bullish on 2020, but Seager—arguably the only success of Zduriencik's recruitment strategy—was a bit more clear-eyed about the goals of the 2020 season: "There's going to be a lot of guys in the clubhouse that don't know things. You have to ask questions and have someone that can answer them." Who has two thumbs, has spent his whole career with Seattle, and looked like he was holding the short end of the answering bat? That guy, the oldest on the team at the ripe old age of 33. "My role is to help all the guys kind of continue to grow and help them along. That benefits me, too...If we improve a lot and we get better quickly, that's great for me."

If 2020 was a season for questions and answers, what better backdrop than a season that is all question marks, where every team is unsettled by COVID risks and safety protocols? It didn't make up for the experience of games played, of course, but maybe guys who didn't know what a cheering stadium sounds like didn't miss it as much. And while sixty games was a disappointment for many athletes at their peaks (such as Trout) who hoped for career-besting performances this year, the scrawny 2020 season may have been a blessing in disguise for a bench full of rookies and otherwise young players who just needed to learn the ropes, stay healthy, and gain experience on the way to better, brighter seasons. For the Mariners, perhaps the worst thing lost was the opportunity for Kyle Lewis to go from hot to cold to hot again—his first month was breathlessly exciting to watch, his second a bit wobbly. If he'd played through three months, four, five, would he have evened out, or would he have run aground? After his early-career knee injuries, the prudent route would be not to wait around to see. And it hardly mattered—despite his slower September, he was still the unanimous pick for Rookie of the Year.

Even if Lewis hadn't redeemed himself in the eyes of the BBWAA, the good thing is that next spring he will be a year older, a year wiser and a year stronger. Same with Evan White, the other rookie of the Mariners' year—the 2017 first-round draft pick, with his impossible wingspan, nabbed a Gold Glove at first base. J.P. Crawford, the shortstop, caught one, too. Both men have work to do at the plate—White was second in the league in strikeouts—but presumably the young infielders were teaching their veteran mentor at third a few things, too.

Seattle riffs off of Rome's seven hills, but the Italian capital's other maxim on city planning is perhaps even more helpful to the Emerald City: "Rome wasn't built in a day." The same could be said for Seattle's wayward, well-meaning baseball franchise—building a team takes time. But it also takes concerted effort, as indicated by the 2020 Tampa Bay Rays. Watching that even younger franchise reach the World Series felt, to Mariners fans, like getting lapped and then lapped again. The Mariners have always wanted to win, but haven't quite acted on it, not in a concerted, coordinated effort. To return to the wall metaphor, the Mariners get stuck about four feet up the climb and can't find another handhold. There are no pegs, no chalk marks for a safe route. No wonder Dipoto dropped off the wall and assumed the slouch of GMs before.

But after so many years—and several front office administrations—of that defeatist posture, of hoping the raw talent, the short game, and some supernatural leaps would get them to October (but knowing it likely wouldn't), maybe the Mariners have finally come to realize there is another way to deal with the wall. Cue the dynamite.

Here's what we learned on March 26, 2000. The great thing about intentional implosion, about dynamite as an element of construction, is that after the dust has settled and the rubble has been cleared, you have a great big empty canvas on which to make your mark. A new stadium gets erected. A new farm system is built—this time, more determinedly so (I'm looking at Jarred Kelenic, Julio Rodríguez, Emerson Hancock and company). Most franchises figure out the up-and-over route to maturity, but Seattleites have gone their own slow, weird way through most things, adolescence included. The Mariners are perhaps, at last, both self-aware and self-empowered, and with that kismet they'll know how to make something out of the clearing.

It feels appropriate to hum Nirvana as we wait. No, not the disaffected anthem of "Teen Spirit"—I'd point surly Seattle fans to Nirvana's third and final album, *In Utero*. The Mariners' has been a long gestation, but if we are to believe Dipoto, it should be coming to a close this season. The anthem of that album? "All Apologies," which opens with the question, "What else should I be?" Maybe the M's finally have an answer to that mournful, frustrated query. That answer: a team that plays in October.

—*Emily Nemens is the author of The Cactus League.*

Part 2: Player Analysis

PLAYER COMMENTS WITH GRAPHS

J.P. Crawford SS
Born: 01/11/95   Age: 26   Bats: L   Throws: R
Height: 6'2"   Weight: 199   Origin: Round 1, 2013 Draft (#16 overall)

YEAR	TEAM	LVL	AGE	PA	R	2B	3B	HR	RBI	BB	K	SB	CS	AVG/OBP/SLG
2018	CLR	HI-A	23	49	8	1	0	1	4	7	14	0	0	.143/.265/.238
2018	LHV	AAA	23	68	6	2	1	1	7	5	17	1	0	.259/.358/.379
2018	PHI	MLB	23	138	17	6	3	3	12	13	37	2	0	.214/.319/.393
2019	TAC	AAA	24	138	20	7	0	3	15	19	25	3	0	.319/.420/.457
2019	SEA	MLB	24	396	43	21	4	7	46	43	83	5	3	.226/.313/.371
2020	SEA	MLB	25	232	33	7	2	2	24	23	39	6	3	.255/.336/.338
2021 FS	SEA	MLB	26	600	76	26	3	13	52	71	121	3	2	.241/.339/.383
2021 DC	SEA	MLB	26	611	77	27	3	13	53	72	123	3	2	.241/.339/.383

Comparables: Andre Rodgers, Julio Lugo, Ricky Gutierrez

Top prospects face a tough grading curve. A 25-year-old shortstop hitting a hair below league average while playing Gold Glove-winning defense should be considered a wild success story. But when you're in your seventh professional season, most of which has been spent well within Top 10 MLB prospect lists, anything less than true stardom can feel like missed potential. At this point it's probably unfair to grade Crawford as a potential Lindorian infield keystone, especially given his Spike Owen-level power. Whether that's what Seattle expected when they acquired him two years ago for Jean Segura is unclear, and also irrelevant. He'll be 26 this year and appears poised to be a highly-capable major league shortstop for years to come. Despite the sport's brutal ecosystem, that's a success for anyone, regardless of hype.

YEAR	TEAM	LVL	AGE	PA	DRC+	BABIP	BRR	FRAA	WARP
2018	CLR	HI-A	23	49	51	.185	0.0	SS(8): -0.6, 3B(3): 0.5	-0.2
2018	LHV	AAA	23	68	83	.350	-1.7	SS(16): 0.2	-0.1
2018	PHI	MLB	23	138	78	.286	0.2	SS(30): 0.6, 3B(13): -0.6	0.2
2019	TAC	AAA	24	138	108	.382	2.6	SS(31): 0.1	1.0
2019	SEA	MLB	24	396	83	.275	-1.9	SS(93): 4.6	1.3
2020	SEA	MLB	25	232	93	.303	2.0	SS(53): 5.0	1.2
2021 FS	SEA	MLB	26	600	100	.291	-0.3	SS 2, 3B 0	2.0
2021 DC	SEA	MLB	26	611	100	.291	-0.3	SS 2	2.0

J.P. Crawford, continued

Batted Ball Distribution

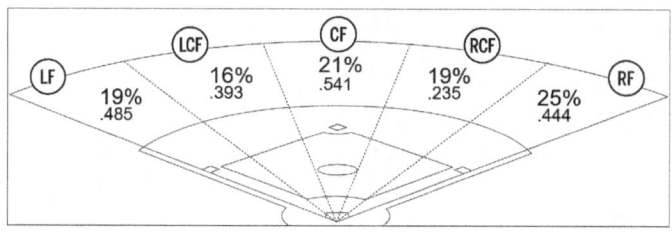

Strike Zone vs LHP   **Strike Zone vs RHP**

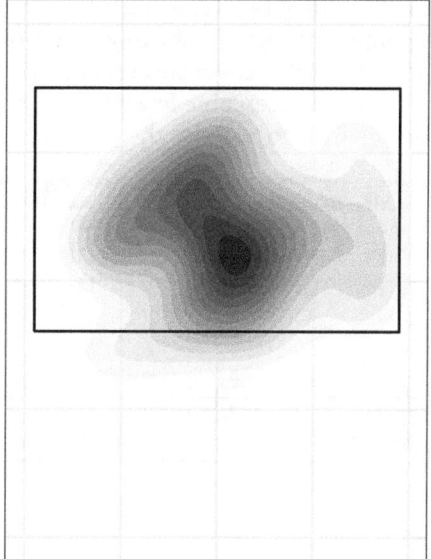

Seattle Mariners 2021

Ty France 3B

Born: 07/13/94 Age: 26 Bats: R Throws: R
Height: 5'11" Weight: 217 Origin: Round 34, 2015 Draft (#1017 overall)

YEAR	TEAM	LVL	AGE	PA	R	2B	3B	HR	RBI	BB	K	SB	CS	AVG/OBP/SLG
2018	SA	AA	23	479	66	22	2	17	77	33	70	3	4	.263/.349/.448
2018	ELP	AAA	23	110	18	8	0	5	19	13	19	0	0	.287/.382/.532
2019	ELP	AAA	24	348	83	27	1	27	89	30	51	1	0	.399/.477/.770
2019	SD	MLB	24	201	20	8	1	7	24	9	49	0	2	.234/.294/.402
2020	SD	MLB	25	61	9	4	0	2	10	5	15	0	0	.309/.377/.491
2020	SEA	MLB	25	94	10	5	1	2	13	6	22	0	0	.302/.362/.453
2021 FS	SEA	MLB	26	600	73	23	1	24	77	39	147	0	1	.245/.321/.431
2021 DC	SEA	MLB	26	464	56	18	1	18	59	30	114	0	1	.245/.321/.431

Comparables: Freddy Garcia, Phil Nevin, Travis Metcalf

Any serious discussion on France should at least mention how tragically close his name comes to giving us the 80-grade spoonerism "Fry Trance". That his wide carriage and non-angular frame would have made this nickname even more apt just drives the knife deeper. Nonetheless, there's plenty to love about the thumping DH/3B. While the 183 DRC+ he posted in Triple-A in 2018 looks like a comical outlier, his above-average offensive profile makes him the first potential Kyle Seager successor Seattle has had in years. At worst, France should provide an acceptable few years at DH until the Mariners sign a 45-year-old Nelson Cruz to push for the 2025 World Series.

YEAR	TEAM	LVL	AGE	PA	DRC+	BABIP	BRR	FRAA	WARP
2018	SA	AA	23	479	121	.276	1.3	3B(101): -7.7, 1B(1): -0.0	0.9
2018	ELP	AAA	23	110	131	.310	0.6	3B(19): 2.8, 1B(9): 0.1	0.9
2019	ELP	AAA	24	348	183	.410	1.0	3B(32): -1.8, 1B(29): -2.3, 2B(15): -2.5	3.7
2019	SD	MLB	24	201	77	.279	0.4	3B(36): -0.6, 2B(21): 2.2, P(2): 0.1	0.3
2020	SD	MLB	25	61	101	.395	0.6	1B(5): 0.4, 3B(2): 0.3	0.2
2020	SEA	MLB	25	94	97	.387	-0.2	2B(10): -0.5, 3B(4): 0.2	0.1
2021 FS	SEA	MLB	26	600	104	.293	-0.8	2B 0, 3B 0	1.4
2021 DC	SEA	MLB	26	464	104	.293	-0.7	2B 0, 3B 0	1.1

Ty France, continued

Batted Ball Distribution

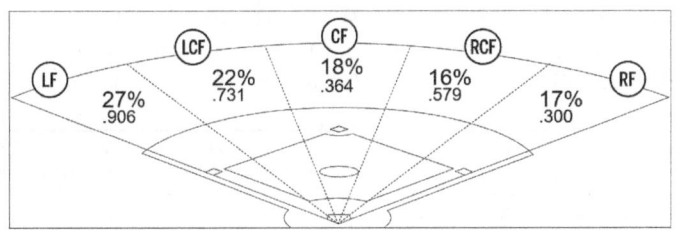

Strike Zone vs LHP   **Strike Zone vs RHP**

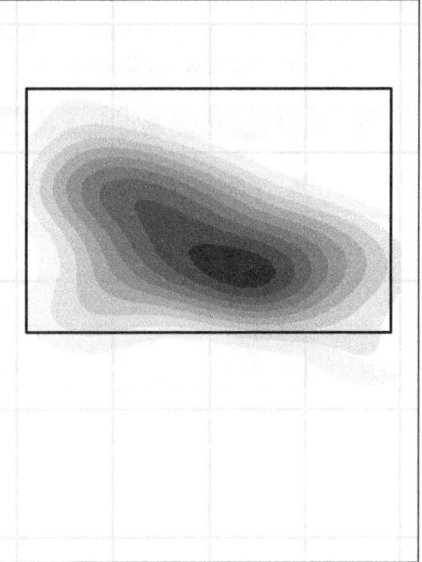

Sam Haggerty 2B

Born: 05/26/94 Age: 27 Bats: S Throws: R
Height: 5'11" Weight: 175 Origin: Round 24, 2015 Draft (#724 overall)

YEAR	TEAM	LVL	AGE	PA	R	2B	3B	HR	RBI	BB	K	SB	CS	AVG/OBP/SLG
2018	AKR	AA	24	351	44	21	5	4	37	57	77	24	7	.243/.373/.396
2019	BRK	SS	25	25	5	3	0	0	4	4	8	0	0	.333/.440/.476
2019	BNG	AA	25	292	39	8	5	2	13	40	78	19	4	.259/.370/.356
2019	SYR	AAA	25	49	9	4	1	1	9	4	10	4	0	.310/.383/.524
2019	NYM	MLB	25	4	2	0	0	0	0	0	3	0	0	.000/.000/.000
2020	SEA	MLB	26	54	7	4	0	1	6	4	16	4	0	.260/.315/.400
2021 FS	SEA	MLB	27	600	67	19	4	10	49	64	191	20	7	.197/.290/.309
2021 DC	SEA	MLB	27	70	7	2	0	1	5	7	22	2	1	.197/.290/.309

Comparables: Ryan Schimpf, Michael Reed, Tyler Goeddel

Haggerty not only profiles as a fringe 25th man on a major league roster, he's theoretically a 26th, 27th, or even a 28th as well. Clearly, he's a man of many talents. One of his legitimate skills is discerning bad pitches, leading to strong walk rates; sadly, one of them is not hitting good pitches, thus poor strikeout rates. Given his sketchy, stopgap defense and doubles-at-best power, Haggerty (whose middle name, we feel compelled to mention, is Onofrio) is probably trending toward 29th or 30th man as his age moves toward 27 and 28.

YEAR	TEAM	LVL	AGE	PA	DRC+	BABIP	BRR	FRAA	WARP
2018	AKR	AA	24	351	115	.314	1.2	3B(41): -5.0, SS(19): -0.3, LF(11): 0.4	0.8
2019	BRK	SS	25	25	117	.538	0.8	3B(2): 0.1, 2B(1): -0.3, SS(1): 0.1	0.2
2019	BNG	AA	25	292	118	.369	4.2	CF(25): 0.2, 2B(23): -1.2, 3B(4): -0.2	1.7
2019	SYR	AAA	25	49	106	.387	-0.6	2B(7): -0.4, LF(5): -0.5, SS(2): -0.0	0.0
2019	NYM	MLB	25	4	57	.000	0.5	2B(1): -0.0, RF(1): 0.0	0.0
2020	SEA	MLB	26	54	95	.364	0.9	LF(10): 2.0, 3B(1): 0.1, RF(1): -0.1	0.3
2021 FS	SEA	MLB	27	600	68	.286	2.0	2B -1, 3B 0	-0.8
2021 DC	SEA	MLB	27	70	68	.286	0.2	2B 0	-0.1

Sam Haggerty, continued

Batted Ball Distribution

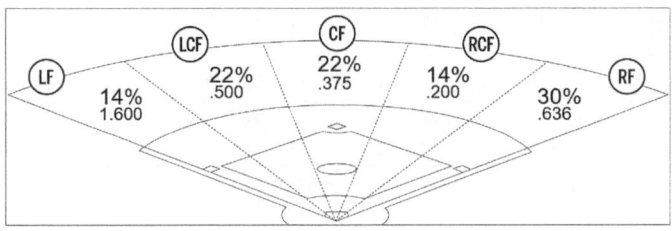

Strike Zone vs LHP   Strike Zone vs RHP

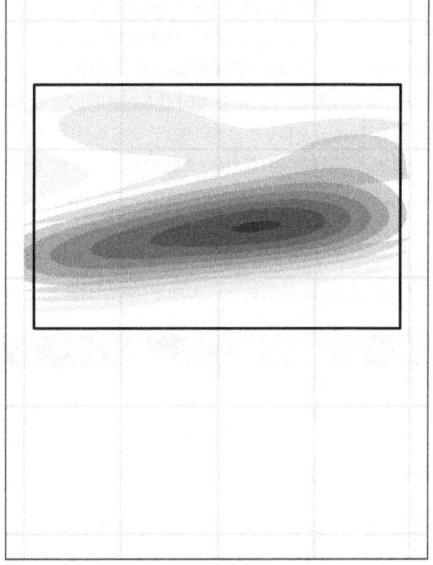

Kyle Lewis CF

Born: 07/13/95 Age: 25 Bats: R Throws: R
Height: 6'4" Weight: 205 Origin: Round 1, 2016 Draft (#11 overall)

YEAR	TEAM	LVL	AGE	PA	R	2B	3B	HR	RBI	BB	K	SB	CS	AVG/OBP/SLG
2018	MOD	HI-A	22	211	21	18	0	5	32	11	55	0	0	.260/.303/.429
2018	ARK	AA	22	152	18	8	0	4	20	17	32	1	0	.220/.309/.371
2019	ARK	AA	23	517	61	25	2	11	62	56	152	3	2	.263/.342/.398
2019	SEA	MLB	23	75	10	5	0	6	13	3	29	0	0	.268/.293/.592
2020	SEA	MLB	24	242	37	3	0	11	28	34	71	5	1	.262/.364/.437
2021 FS	SEA	MLB	25	600	73	24	2	23	74	61	188	0	1	.237/.319/.425
2021 DC	SEA	MLB	25	578	70	23	1	23	71	59	181	0	1	.237/.319/.425

Comparables: Ramón Laureano, Joc Pederson, Adolfo Phillips

After a catastrophic knee injury suffered when a catcher (in Single-A) blocked the plate, the former Golden Spikes Award winner spent years slowly regaining his timing and athleticism. The pace of that recovery led to many assuming a big league career wasn't in the cards. Lewis persevered, however, and after a flashy, home run-filed cup of coffee, he was handed the everyday center field job for 2020. He ran with it like Usain Bolt in London, improving his plate discipline, hitting for power, and moving on that surgically-repaired knee well enough to play a perfectly acceptable center field. The year resulted in both a unanimous Rookie of the Year award selection and some pretty significant questions about this future, given a severe second-half slump (.545 OPS). Pitchers acclimated to his fast start, and he responded by hitting the ball harder than ever, upwards, converting line drives to fly balls. The short season probably interrupted the usual rhythm of adjustment and readjustment for every young hitter. It also probably demonstrated what Lewis is: streaky as hell, and a quality player when it's all given time to average out.

YEAR	TEAM	LVL	AGE	PA	DRC+	BABIP	BRR	FRAA	WARP
2018	MOD	HI-A	22	211	103	.333	0.3	CF(23): -3.1, RF(11): -0.7, LF(2): 0.1	-0.3
2018	ARK	AA	22	152	90	.255	-2.0	CF(29): -2.6, RF(1): -0.0	-0.6
2019	ARK	AA	23	517	111	.367	-3.3	LF(49): 0.1, CF(36): -4.0, RF(15): -1.2	0.8
2019	SEA	MLB	23	75	84	.351	0.8	RF(17): 0.0, CF(2): 0.1	0.1
2020	SEA	MLB	24	242	108	.341	1.4	CF(57): 0.2	1.0
2021 FS	SEA	MLB	25	600	102	.319	-0.7	CF 1, RF 0	1.9
2021 DC	SEA	MLB	25	578	102	.319	-0.7	CF 1, RF 0	1.9

Kyle Lewis, continued

Batted Ball Distribution

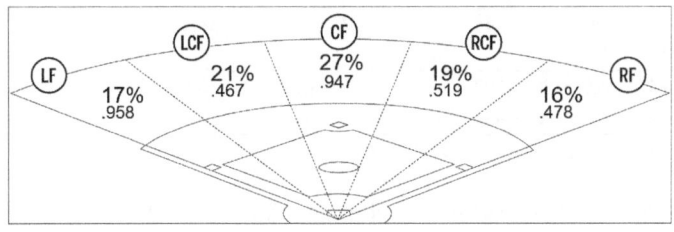

Strike Zone vs LHP **Strike Zone vs RHP**

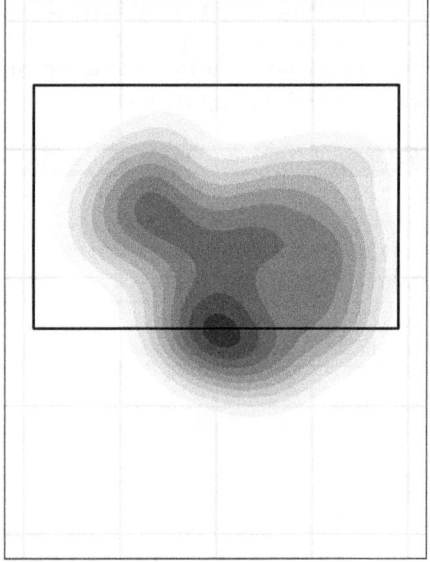

José Marmolejos 1B

Born: 01/02/93 Age: 28 Bats: L Throws: L
Height: 6'2" Weight: 239 Origin: International Free Agent, 2011

YEAR	TEAM	LVL	AGE	PA	R	2B	3B	HR	RBI	BB	K	SB	CS	AVG/OBP/SLG
2018	SYR	AAA	25	539	52	25	1	8	57	39	97	0	0	.266/.319/.369
2019	HBG	AA	26	43	8	2	0	2	10	4	6	0	0	.308/.372/.513
2019	FRE	AAA	26	382	53	29	2	16	63	28	80	1	0	.315/.366/.545
2020	SEA	MLB	27	115	12	4	0	6	18	7	32	0	1	.206/.261/.411
2021 FS	SEA	MLB	28	600	63	25	2	21	69	40	163	0	0	.232/.291/.403
2021 DC	SEA	MLB	28	354	37	14	1	12	41	24	96	0	0	.232/.291/.403

Comparables: Scott Thorman, Garrett Jones, Dayan Viciedo

There's a noticeable dissonance between the abnormality of the 2020 season and the traditional abnormality that was the Seattle Mariners roster; the twin phenomena conspired to make a lot of major league dreams true. One of those was Marmolejos, a thumping first baseman who finally made it to the show in this 10th season in professional baseball ... starting Opening Day in left field. After a brutal 3-for-29 start, the longtime farmhand made way for other die rolls, though he did return in the second half with an .801 OPS. Given the impending arrival of real outfield prospects and the fact that he really shouldn't be playing the field anyway, Marmolejos will probably remain bound to 2020, a sliver of a year's fever dream. But one of the less horrific parts, perhaps?

YEAR	TEAM	LVL	AGE	PA	DRC+	BABIP	BRR	FRAA	WARP
2018	SYR	AAA	25	539	105	.313	-2.1	1B(73): -1.3, RF(30): -1.6, LF(21): -2.5	-0.4
2019	HBG	AA	26	43	134	.323	0.3	LF(7): -0.2	0.3
2019	FRE	AAA	26	382	112	.370	-3.9	1B(48): 0.7, LF(23): 1.4, RF(14): -0.8	1.0
2020	SEA	MLB	27	115	85	.232	-0.2	LF(18): 0.6, 1B(5): -0.3, RF(2): 0.1	0.0
2021 FS	SEA	MLB	28	600	85	.291	-0.8	LF 0, 1B 0	-0.1
2021 DC	SEA	MLB	28	354	85	.291	-0.5	LF 0, 1B 0	-0.1

José Marmolejos, continued

Batted Ball Distribution

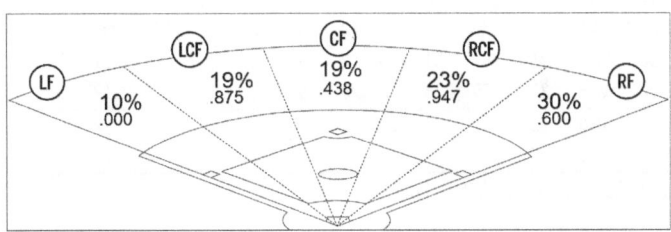

Strike Zone vs LHP   Strike Zone vs RHP

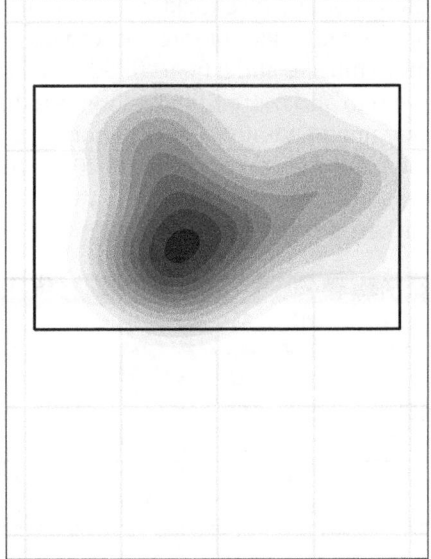

Dylan Moore OF

Born: 08/02/92   Age: 28   Bats: R   Throws: R
Height: 6'0"   Weight: 185   Origin: Round 7, 2015 Draft (#198 overall)

YEAR	TEAM	LVL	AGE	PA	R	2B	3B	HR	RBI	BB	K	SB	CS	AVG/OBP/SLG
2018	BLX	AA	25	91	12	7	3	3	18	7	16	6	1	.373/.429/.639
2018	RMV	AAA	25	363	58	24	6	11	40	28	52	17	6	.280/.346/.492
2019	TAC	AAA	26	35	3	0	0	0	7	3	3	2	1	.172/.294/.172
2019	SEA	MLB	26	282	31	14	2	9	28	25	92	11	9	.206/.302/.389
2020	SEA	MLB	27	159	26	9	0	8	17	14	43	12	5	.255/.358/.496
2021 FS	SEA	MLB	28	600	76	27	2	21	65	49	173	17	8	.223/.310/.402
2021 DC	SEA	MLB	28	507	64	22	1	17	55	41	146	14	7	.223/.310/.402

Comparables: Billy Ashley, Danny Walton, Pete Incaviglia

    The Jerry Dipoto Mariners have earned a bit of a reputation for doing what the kids used to call "galaxy braining." For those of you fortunate enough to not have your brains disordered by social media, you'll recognize it by its ancestral term: out-thinking the room. This is to say that in 2018, when Seattle gave a major league contract to a lifetime minor leaguer entering his age-27 season, there were some chuckles at the team's expense. After a 2019 that justified a lot of those chuckles Moore showed up to the abbreviated 2020 campaign with more muscle and a heart filled with ill-intent towards baseballs. Moore used them to add more than two miles to his average exit velocity, 100 points to his slugging percentage, and 40 points to his DRC+. Add in some defensive utility (he played seven positions in 2020), and Moore is either a fun story in a weird season or another in a moderate but steadily growing series of developmental success stories for Seattle.

YEAR	TEAM	LVL	AGE	PA	DRC+	BABIP	BRR	FRAA	WARP
2018	BLX	AA	25	91	157	.438	-0.4	2B(9): -0.6, 1B(7): -0.8, SS(3): -0.3	0.3
2018	RMV	AAA	25	363	110	.303	3.3	3B(54): 0.2, 2B(25): -2.3, 1B(9): 0.3	1.3
2019	TAC	AAA	26	35	49	.192	0.3	SS(3): -0.1, 2B(2): 0.2, 3B(1): -0.0	-0.1
2019	SEA	MLB	26	282	79	.288	-1.1	SS(31): 0.1, LF(31): 2.1, 2B(18): 1.5	0.4
2020	SEA	MLB	27	159	117	.314	0.4	LF(13): -1.0, RF(13): 1.4, 2B(10): 0.6	0.9
2021 FS	SEA	MLB	28	600	94	.289	1.3	2B 0, RF 1	1.4
2021 DC	SEA	MLB	28	507	94	.289	1.1	2B 0, RF 1	1.2

Dylan Moore, continued

Batted Ball Distribution

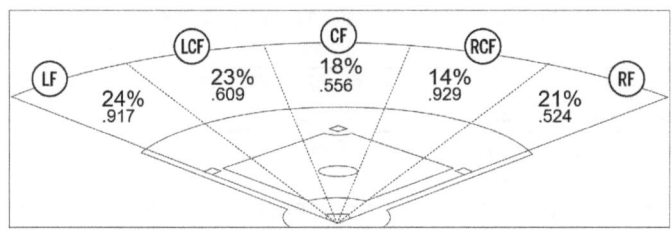

Strike Zone vs LHP   Strike Zone vs RHP

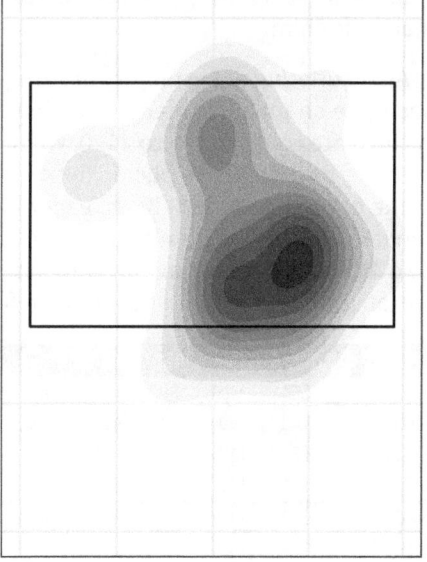

Kyle Seager 3B

Born: 11/03/87   Age: 33   Bats: L   Throws: R
Height: 6'0"   Weight: 216   Origin: Round 3, 2009 Draft (#82 overall)

YEAR	TEAM	LVL	AGE	PA	R	2B	3B	HR	RBI	BB	K	SB	CS	AVG/OBP/SLG
2018	SEA	MLB	30	630	62	36	1	22	78	38	138	2	2	.221/.273/.400
2019	TAC	AAA	31	42	5	2	0	0	7	3	7	0	0	.256/.310/.308
2019	SEA	MLB	31	443	55	19	1	23	63	44	86	2	2	.239/.321/.468
2020	SEA	MLB	32	248	35	12	0	9	40	32	33	5	0	.241/.355/.433
2021 FS	SEA	MLB	33	600	73	29	1	23	77	59	108	2	2	.245/.331/.438
2021 DC	SEA	MLB	33	577	71	28	1	22	74	56	104	2	2	.245/.331/.438

Comparables: Ryan Zimmerman, Adrián Beltré, Sean Berry

Kyle Seager is a player defined by competence and its disparate narrative spins. From 2011-2013, he was Dustin Ackley's College Teammate, an afterthought with little pop and utility player upside. From 2014-2016, he was a quiet star on a contending team, thriving behind the supernova talents and personalities of Félix Hernández, Robinson Canó, and Nelson Cruz. From 2017-2020, he has been "overpaid," an aging anchor with a contract and clubhouse personality the team would happily rid itself of, if only there were a market for him.

After suffering a wrist injury in spring training and a slow first half in 2019, Seager re-shaped his offense, posting a second-half wRC+ of 129. That success at the plate continued into 2020, when this reminder of its past was arguably Seattle's best offensive player. In fact, over his past 162 games (stretching back to the doom-filled 2018) Kyle Seager has posted a line of .250/.329/.470, eerily similar to his career numbers of .257/.325/.445. He's Kyle Seager again, same as he ever was: a 3-to-5 win player to set your watch to, and despite his many narratives, the best third baseman in franchise history.

YEAR	TEAM	LVL	AGE	PA	DRC+	BABIP	BRR	FRAA	WARP
2018	SEA	MLB	30	630	90	.251	-1.6	3B(154): 11.2, 2B(1): -0.0	2.5
2019	TAC	AAA	31	42	70	.312	-0.7	3B(5): 0.0	-0.1
2019	SEA	MLB	31	443	113	.248	-2.4	3B(104): -0.2	2.2
2020	SEA	MLB	32	248	130	.240	1.9	3B(53): 2.4	1.8
2021 FS	SEA	MLB	33	600	107	.268	-0.7	3B 1, 2B 0	1.8
2021 DC	SEA	MLB	33	577	107	.268	-0.7	3B 1	1.7

Kyle Seager, continued

Batted Ball Distribution

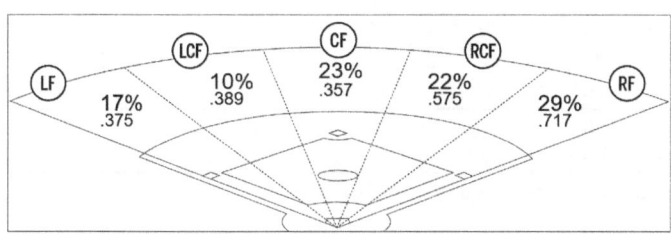

Strike Zone vs LHP   Strike Zone vs RHP

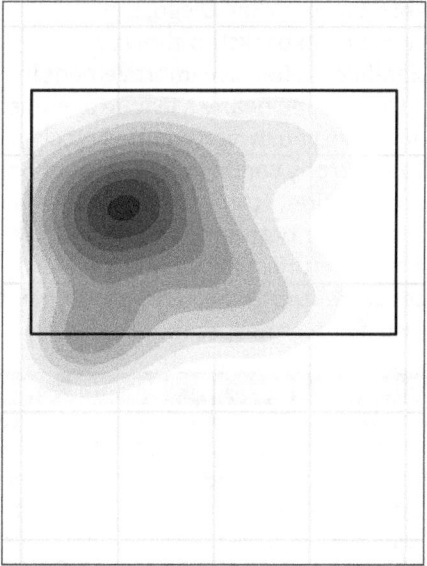

Seattle Mariners 2021

Luis Torrens C

Born: 05/02/96 Age: 25 Bats: R Throws: R
Height: 6'0" Weight: 208 Origin: International Free Agent, 2013

YEAR	TEAM	LVL	AGE	PA	R	2B	3B	HR	RBI	BB	K	SB	CS	AVG/OBP/SLG
2018	LE	HI-A	22	515	62	36	3	6	73	26	77	1	1	.280/.320/.406
2019	AMA	AA	23	397	50	23	1	15	62	42	67	1	2	.300/.373/.500
2019	SD	MLB	23	16	2	1	0	0	0	2	6	0	0	.214/.312/.286
2020	SEA	MLB	24	65	5	4	0	1	6	6	13	0	0	.254/.323/.373
2020	SD	MLB	24	13	0	1	0	0	0	1	2	0	0	.273/.333/.364
2021 FS	SEA	MLB	25	600	65	28	1	15	63	52	134	0	1	.236/.308/.384
2021 DC	SEA	MLB	25	312	34	14	0	8	32	27	70	0	0	.236/.308/.384

Comparables: Nick Hundley, Ryan Lavarnway, Blake Swihart

YEAR	TEAM	P. COUNT	FRM RUNS	BLK RUNS	THRW RUNS	TOT RUNS
2019	SD	495	-0.1	0.4		0.3
2019	AMA	12535	-2.8	0.0	5.2	2.5
2020	SD	597	-0.5	-0.1	0.0	-0.6
2020	SEA	2281	-1.9	-0.3	0.0	-2.2
2021	SEA	12025	-10.0	-1.8	0.0	-11.8
2021	SEA	12025	-10.0	-1.5	0.0	-11.5

A recurring theme of the 2020 Mariners was "not bad given what was expected, which was nothing." Torrens certainly fits the mold. A midseason acquisition in the trade that sent Austin Nola to San Diego, the Venezuelan backstop showed significant offensive improvement in 2020, posting nearly a league average offensive line, which coupled nicely with his nearly average defensive line. With Tom Murphy coming off injury and Cal Raleigh pegged the future by the organization, Torrens most likely looks to spend 2021 shuffling up and down the I-5 corridor between Tacoma and Seattle. That sounds bleak but recent infrastructure improvements have made the freeway interchange much more convenient, and the nearby casino has a new gaming and conference center. Also, food is cheaper in Tacoma.

YEAR	TEAM	LVL	AGE	PA	DRC+	BABIP	BRR	FRAA	WARP
2018	LE	HI-A	22	515	100	.318	1.8	C(85): 1.0, 1B(3): 0.0	0.8
2019	AMA	AA	23	397	134	.331	-2.6	C(85): 3.0, 1B(1): 0.2	3.1
2019	SD	MLB	23	16	74	.375	0.4	C(4): 0.4	0.1
2020	SEA	MLB	24	65	91	.311	-0.3	C(17): 0.0	-0.2
2020	SD	MLB	24	13	94	.333	-0.3	C(7): -0.0	0.0
2021 FS	SEA	MLB	25	600	89	.286	-0.9	C -16, 1B 0	-0.1
2021 DC	SEA	MLB	25	312	89	.286	-0.5	C -11	-0.3

Luis Torrens, continued

Batted Ball Distribution

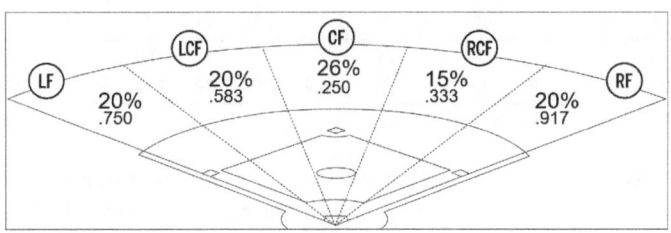

Strike Zone vs LHP   Strike Zone vs RHP

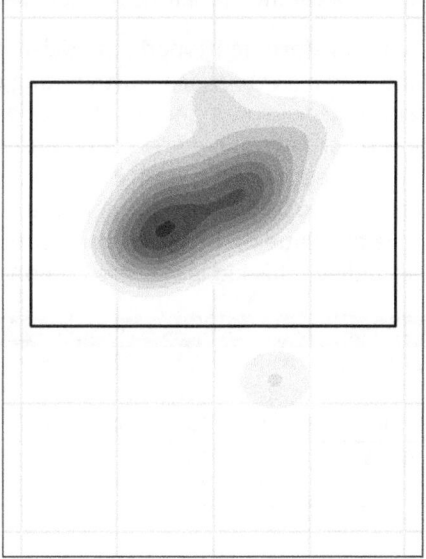

Evan White 1B

Born: 04/26/96 Age: 25 Bats: R Throws: L
Height: 6'3" Weight: 220 Origin: Round 1, 2017 Draft (#17 overall)

YEAR	TEAM	LVL	AGE	PA	R	2B	3B	HR	RBI	BB	K	SB	CS	AVG/OBP/SLG
2018	MOD	HI-A	22	538	72	27	7	11	66	52	103	4	3	.303/.375/.458
2019	ARK	AA	23	400	61	13	2	18	55	29	92	2	0	.293/.350/.488
2020	SEA	MLB	24	202	19	7	0	8	26	18	84	1	2	.176/.252/.346
2021 FS	SEA	MLB	25	600	69	24	2	25	75	43	218	0	1	.227/.289/.417
2021 DC	SEA	MLB	25	540	62	22	2	22	67	39	196	0	1	.227/.289/.417

Comparables: Brad Eldred, Billy Ashley, Nick Evans

Long ballyhooed as the best defensive first base prospect in memory, White delivered on that side of the ball, winning the first of likely many Gold Glove awards and displaying a level of athleticism rarely seen around a position typically manned by your Lukes Voit and Pauls Konerko. Unfortunately for White and the Mariners, the other parts of his scouting profile also proved accurate. Those "other parts" expressed concern about his ability to hit major league pitching, and a 65 DRC+ and 42% K-rate isn't going to work for a strong-defensive catcher, let alone a first baseman.

White's aforementioned athleticism fuels above average raw power at the plate, and it's very much worth noting he rebounded from "disastrous" at the start of the season to merely "below league average" the rest of the way. The tools that made him a first-round pick flash all the time, and there's always that sweet, sweet defense, even if it feels a bit wasted at baseball's most fungible defensive position. The Mariners will give him every opportunity in 2021 to prove the value of the latter, and continue to progress with the former. It's clear they believe this kid is one in a million.

YEAR	TEAM	LVL	AGE	PA	DRC+	BABIP	BRR	FRAA	WARP
2018	MOD	HI-A	22	538	144	.363	-0.5	1B(106): 5.5	2.1
2019	ARK	AA	23	400	153	.346	1.1	1B(88): -5.3	1.9
2020	SEA	MLB	24	202	65	.264	-0.4	1B(54): -1.3	-0.8
2021 FS	SEA	MLB	25	600	90	.325	-0.7	1B -1	-0.1
2021 DC	SEA	MLB	25	540	90	.325	-0.6	1B 0	0.0

Evan White, continued

Batted Ball Distribution

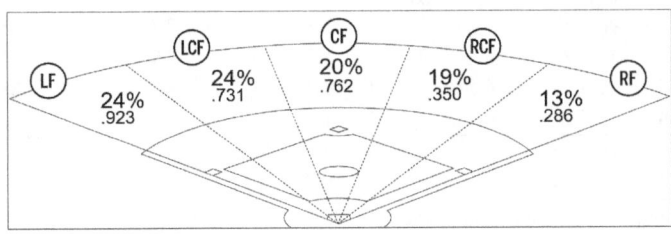

Strike Zone vs LHP   **Strike Zone vs RHP**

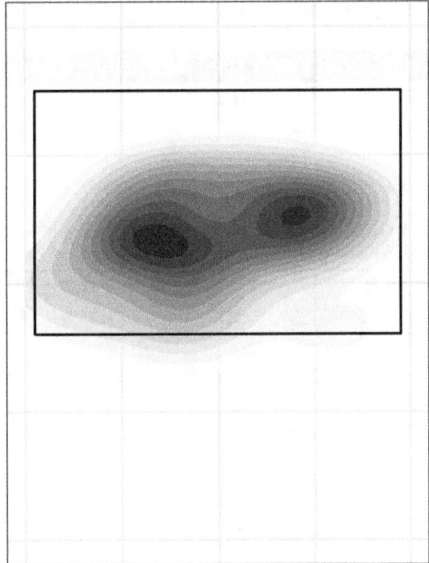

Robert Dugger RHP

Born: 07/03/95   Age: 26   Bats: R   Throws: R
Height: 6'0"   Weight: 198   Origin: Round 18, 2016 Draft (#537 overall)

YEAR	TEAM	LVL	AGE	W	L	SV	G	GS	IP	H	HR	BB/9	K/9	K	GB%	BABIP
2018	JUP	HI-A	22	3	1	0	7	7	41^1	40	2	1.5	7.4	34	56.3%	.309
2018	JAX	AA	22	7	6	0	18	18	109^1	100	13	3.0	8.8	107	34.9%	.299
2019	JAX	AA	23	6	6	0	13	13	70^2	57	6	2.7	9.3	73	45.0%	.282
2019	NO	AAA	23	2	4	0	10	10	53^1	74	12	2.9	8.3	49	36.7%	.376
2019	MIA	MLB	23	0	4	0	7	7	34^1	33	6	4.5	6.6	25	38.5%	.265
2020	MIA	MLB	24	0	0	0	4	1	10^2	21	5	2.5	3.4	4	30.6%	.364
2021 FS	SEA	MLB	25	2	3	0	57	0	50	51	9	3.5	7.2	39	37.2%	.286
2021 DC	SEA	MLB	25	2	2	0	46	0	11.7	12	2	3.5	7.2	9	37.2%	.286

Comparables: Jorge Alcala, Justin Dunn, Bobby Parnell

A somewhat promising back-end pitching prospect in the before times, Dugger's 2020 claim to fame was as the spot starter for José Ureña in the fateful July 26 game that Miami inexplicably played as their COVID outbreak was starting to spiral. Dugger was claimed off waivers by the Mariners (his original team) in December.

YEAR	TEAM	LVL	AGE	WHIP	ERA	DRA-	WARP	MPH	FB%	WHF	CSP
2018	JUP	HI-A	22	1.14	2.40	77	0.8				
2018	JAX	AA	22	1.24	3.79	113	0.0				
2019	JAX	AA	23	1.10	3.31	80	0.9				
2019	NO	AAA	23	1.71	7.59	174	-0.9				
2019	MIA	MLB	23	1.46	5.77	130	-0.2	91.7	59.2%	22.3%	
2020	MIA	MLB	24	2.25	12.66	180	-0.4	93.9	53.8%	11.3%	
2021 FS	SEA	MLB	25	1.43	5.22	115	-0.2	92.5	57.2%	18.4%	45.7%
2021 DC	SEA	MLB	25	1.43	5.22	115	0.0	92.5	57.2%	18.4%	45.7%

Robert Dugger, continued

Pitch Shape vs LHH

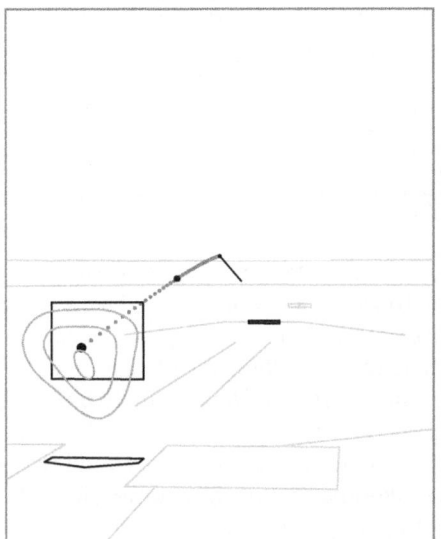

Pitch Shape vs RHH

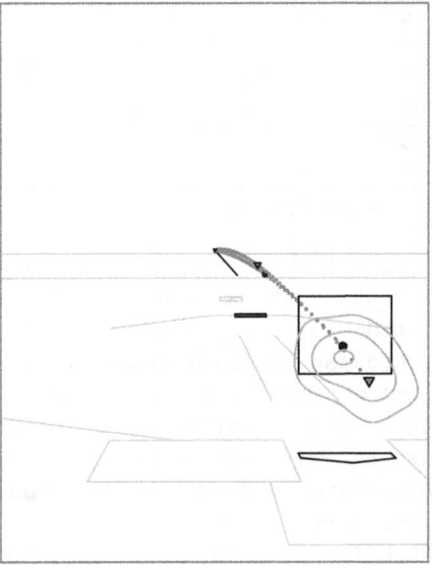

Type	Frequency	Velocity	H Movement	V Movement
● Fastball	42.9%	92.2 [99]	-8.3 [92]	-14.5 [102]
□ Sinker	10.8%	91.8 [97]	-13.9 [94]	-19 [105]
▽ Slider	26.9%	81.8 [91]	4 [95]	-37.2 [90]
◇ Curveball	16.5%	75.8 [89]	9.5 [108]	-50.8 [95]

Seattle Mariners 2021

Justin Dunn   RHP

Born: 09/22/95   Age: 25   Bats: R   Throws: R
Height: 6'2"   Weight: 185   Origin: Round 1, 2016 Draft (#19 overall)

YEAR	TEAM	LVL	AGE	W	L	SV	G	GS	IP	H	HR	BB/9	K/9	K	GB%	BABIP
2018	STL	HI-A	22	2	3	0	9	9	45²	43	2	3.0	10.1	51	39.8%	.331
2018	BNG	AA	22	6	5	0	15	15	89²	85	7	3.7	10.5	105	43.8%	.353
2019	ARK	AA	23	9	5	0	25	25	131²	118	13	2.7	10.8	158	37.5%	.314
2019	SEA	MLB	23	0	0	0	4	4	6²	2	0	12.2	6.8	5	43.8%	.125
2020	SEA	MLB	24	4	1	0	10	10	45²	31	10	6.1	7.5	38	32.3%	.179
2021 FS	SEA	MLB	25	9	9	0	26	26	150	141	27	4.8	8.7	145	35.5%	.281
2021 DC	SEA	MLB	25	6	7	0	24	22	108.7	102	20	4.8	8.7	105	35.5%	.281

Comparables: Robert Dugger, Jordan Yamamoto, T.J. Zeuch

  Some hurlers make pitching look easy, a simple, metronomic, back-and-forth activity with the occasional slow pirouette to watch a teammate field a grounder or drift under a lazy fly ball, but mostly just a calisthenics-heavy game of catch with a man dressed like a ninja turtle. Others make pitching look like Roger Murtaugh in *Lethal Weapon 2*; sitting on a toilet, sweating, desperate to be anywhere else, and hoping not to die. Dunn is one of the latter. The inconsistency of his command and velocity lead to high pitch counts and low-inning starts, without the fun eight-pitch strikeouts that usually come with those. Coming into Dunn's age-26 season the bullpen looks more and more likely, though the raw stuff still provides hope of a late-blooming back-end starter hiding in there somewhere.

YEAR	TEAM	LVL	AGE	WHIP	ERA	DRA-	WARP	MPH	FB%	WHF	CSP
2018	STL	HI-A	22	1.27	2.36	71	1.0				
2018	BNG	AA	22	1.36	4.22	73	1.9				
2019	ARK	AA	23	1.19	3.55	94	0.6				
2019	SEA	MLB	23	1.65	2.70	109	0.0	94.1	58.8%	22.2%	
2020	SEA	MLB	24	1.36	4.34	161	-1.1	93.0	54.8%	22.2%	
2021 FS	SEA	MLB	25	1.47	5.14	112	0.5	93.1	55.2%	22.2%	45.1%
2021 DC	SEA	MLB	25	1.47	5.14	112	0.3	93.1	55.2%	22.2%	45.1%

Justin Dunn, continued

Pitch Shape vs LHH

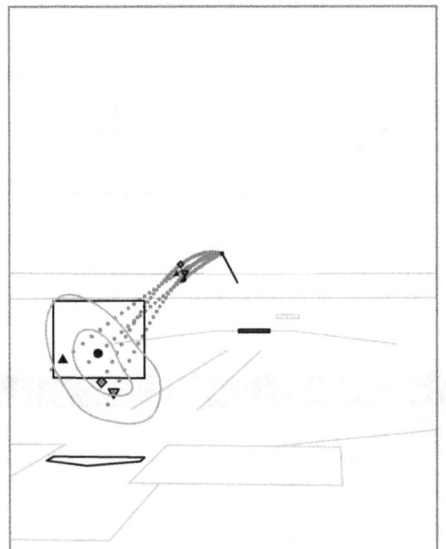

Pitch Shape vs RHH

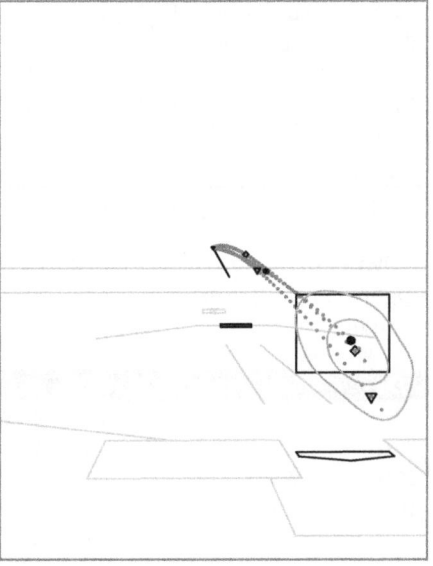

Type	Frequency	Velocity	H Movement	V Movement
● Fastball	54.2%	91.3 [96]	-7.3 [97]	-14.3 [102]
▲ Changeup	6.1%	87.2 [108]	-10.7 [105]	-22 [115]
▽ Slider	15.2%	83.1 [96]	6 [103]	-36.4 [92]
◇ Curveball	23.7%	79.5 [104]	12.9 [122]	-37.7 [124]

Joey Gerber   RHP

Born: 05/03/97   Age: 24   Bats: R   Throws: R
Height: 6'4"   Weight: 215   Origin: Round 8, 2018 Draft (#238 overall)

YEAR	TEAM	LVL	AGE	W	L	SV	G	GS	IP	H	HR	BB/9	K/9	K	GB%	BABIP
2018	EVE	SS	21	1	0	6	13	0	14	9	0	3.9	13.5	21	59.3%	.333
2018	CLI	LO-A	21	0	0	2	9	0	11^2	9	0	3.9	17.0	22	35.0%	.450
2019	MOD	HI-A	22	0	2	8	25	0	26	17	0	4.2	13.5	39	37.5%	.309
2019	ARK	AA	22	1	2	0	19	0	22^2	21	2	2.8	11.9	30	37.9%	.345
2020	SEA	MLB	23	1	1	0	17	0	15^2	13	1	2.9	3.4	6	42.0%	.245
2021 FS	SEA	MLB	24	2	2	0	57	0	50	47	8	4.1	9.0	49	40.1%	.289
2021 DC	SEA	MLB	24	1	1	0	34	0	35.7	33	5	4.1	9.0	35	40.1%	.289

Comparables: Jose Santiago, Randy Moffitt, Miles Mikolas

Owner of a mid-90's fastball and a moderately amusing Twitter account (@gerb_nation), Gerber has one publicly-distinguishing feature. It is not the fastball.

YEAR	TEAM	LVL	AGE	WHIP	ERA	DRA-	WARP	MPH	FB%	WHF	CSP
2018	EVE	SS	21	1.07	1.93	156	-0.4				
2018	CLI	LO-A	21	1.20	2.31	45	0.4				
2019	MOD	HI-A	22	1.12	3.46	49	0.7				
2019	ARK	AA	22	1.24	1.59	88	0.1				
2020	SEA	MLB	23	1.15	4.02	125	-0.1	95.7	65.2%	20.2%	
2021 FS	SEA	MLB	24	1.40	4.64	103	0.1	95.7	65.2%	20.2%	51.0%
2021 DC	SEA	MLB	24	1.40	4.64	103	0.1	95.7	65.2%	20.2%	51.0%

Joey Gerber, continued

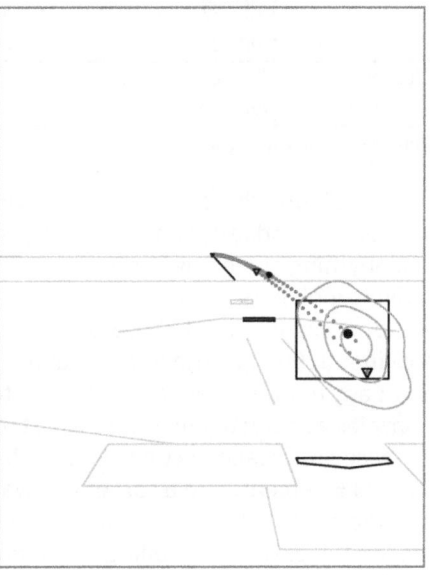

Type	Frequency	Velocity	H Movement	V Movement
● Fastball	65.2%	93.5 [103]	-11 [79]	-14.4 [102]
▽ Slider	34.8%	83.9 [100]	4.1 [96]	-29 [114]

Marco Gonzales LHP

Born: 02/16/92 Age: 29 Bats: L Throws: L
Height: 6'1" Weight: 197 Origin: Round 1, 2013 Draft (#19 overall)

YEAR	TEAM	LVL	AGE	W	L	SV	G	GS	IP	H	HR	BB/9	K/9	K	GB%	BABIP
2018	SEA	MLB	26	13	9	0	29	29	166²	172	17	1.7	7.8	145	44.7%	.320
2019	SEA	MLB	27	16	13	0	34	34	203	210	23	2.5	6.5	147	41.2%	.295
2020	SEA	MLB	28	7	2	0	11	11	69²	59	8	0.9	8.3	64	37.6%	.263
2021 FS	SEA	MLB	29	9	8	0	26	26	150	152	26	2.1	8.0	133	39.4%	.294
2021 DC	SEA	MLB	29	11	9	0	29	29	174.7	177	30	2.1	8.0	155	39.4%	.294

Comparables: Kevin Gausman, Jon Gray, Sean Manaea

If there's one thing Jerry Dipoto loves more than trading, it's talking. The man has his own podcast, and he uses it to offer rose-tinted projections on anyone and anything graced by Mariner teal. The experience can be simultaneously a thrilling look behind the scenes of a major league baseball front office, and a tiresome exercise in PR. Dipoto's relentless hype, combined with a fastball that red-lines at 90 mph and a DRA that has long insisted, "This is all going to fall apart any minute now," have contributed to the delayed acknowledgment of Gonzales as a quality major league starting pitcher. The former first-round pick increased his usage of cutter and fastball in 2020 to set a career high strikeout rate (23.5 percent) and a career low walk rate (2.9 percent). When a player's K/BB ratio starts getting into prime Cliff Lee territory, it's time to start revising those back-end starter ceiling projections. That said, unless Gonzales enrolls in the James Paxton School of Magical Velocity Acquisition, it's hard to imagine him getting much better than he was in 2020. Even with some mild regression in 2021, though, he has proven himself the wheat in Jerry Dipoto's mountains of verbal chaff.

YEAR	TEAM	LVL	AGE	WHIP	ERA	DRA-	WARP	MPH	FB%	WHF	CSP
2018	SEA	MLB	26	1.22	4.00	79	3.3	91.6	32.5%	21.1%	
2019	SEA	MLB	27	1.31	3.99	118	0.0	90.2	39.6%	18.0%	
2020	SEA	MLB	28	0.95	3.10	89	1.0	89.8	45.2%	19.7%	
2021 FS	SEA	MLB	29	1.25	4.22	98	1.6	90.4	39.6%	19.1%	51.2%
2021 DC	SEA	MLB	29	1.25	4.22	98	1.9	90.4	39.6%	19.1%	51.2%

Marco Gonzales, continued

Pitch Shape vs LHH	Pitch Shape vs RHH
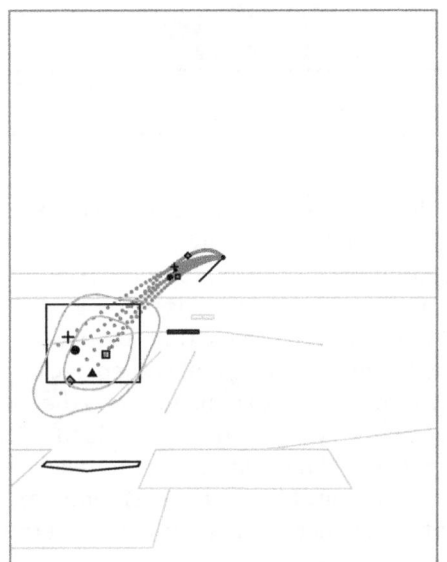	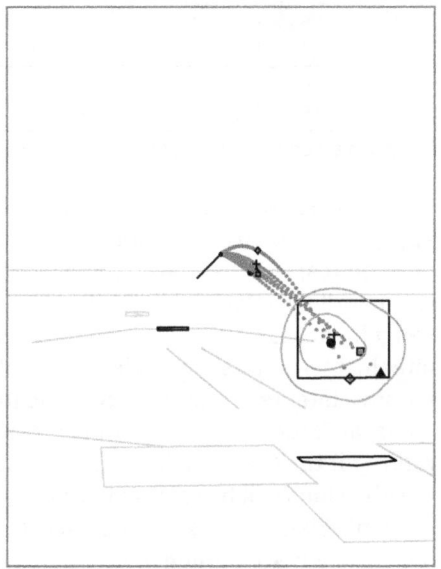

Type	Frequency	Velocity	H Movement	V Movement
● Fastball	24.0%	88.4 [87]	8.5 [92]	-15.3 [100]
☐ Sinker	21.2%	88.4 [79]	11.1 [114]	-17.6 [109]
+ Cutter	24.3%	85 [79]	-0.1 [88]	-24.5 [99]
▲ Changeup	14.4%	80.8 [83]	15 [83]	-29.5 [95]
◇ Curveball	16.1%	75.5 [88]	-7.9 [102]	-55.8 [83]

Kendall Graveman RHP

Born: 12/21/90 Age: 30 Bats: R Throws: R
Height: 6'2" Weight: 200 Origin: Round 8, 2013 Draft (#235 overall)

YEAR	TEAM	LVL	AGE	W	L	SV	G	GS	IP	H	HR	BB/9	K/9	K	GB%	BABIP
2018	NAS	AAA	27	2	1	0	4	4	24	35	3	2.6	6.0	16	54.9%	.405
2018	OAK	MLB	27	1	5	0	7	7	34^1	44	9	3.4	7.1	27	56.4%	.324
2020	SEA	MLB	29	1	3	0	11	2	18^2	15	2	3.9	7.2	15	48.1%	.250
2021 FS	SEA	MLB	30	2	3	6	57	0	50	51	8	3.3	7.5	41	48.9%	.296
2021 DC	SEA	MLB	30	2	3	6	58	0	59.7	61	9	3.3	7.5	49	48.9%	.296

Comparables: Chris Stratton, Jordan Lyles, Luke Hochevar

After a first act you could call "Charlie Morton: The Early Years," Graveman appeared in Peoria after more than a year missed from Tommy John surgery, and spent spring training looking like "Charlie Morton: The Later Years". Gone was middling velocity, low-strikeout pitcher from Oakland. In his place: a vengeful demon, flinging 97 mph two-seamers at the corners. Unfortunately, after just two starts, he landed on the IL with what was originally called neck spasms, later revealed to be complications from a benign bone tumor in the spine, an issue that will eventually demand surgery. Graveman was able to return for the season's final month, but fatigue and pain limited him to relief. Baseball fans will be rooting hard for him to get fully healthy for 2021, both for humanitarian reasons, and because that two-seamer burning the crisp desert air was really something to see.

YEAR	TEAM	LVL	AGE	WHIP	ERA	DRA-	WARP	MPH	FB%	WHF	CSP
2018	NAS	AAA	27	1.75	4.50	96	0.3				
2018	OAK	MLB	27	1.66	7.60	120	0.0	95.7	57.1%	19.6%	
2020	SEA	MLB	29	1.23	5.79	106	0.1	97.7	68.1%	18.6%	
2021 FS	SEA	MLB	30	1.40	4.80	107	0.0	96.9	63.8%	19.0%	45.7%
2021 DC	SEA	MLB	30	1.40	4.80	107	0.2	96.9	63.8%	19.0%	45.7%

Kendall Graveman, continued

Pitch Shape vs LHH	Pitch Shape vs RHH
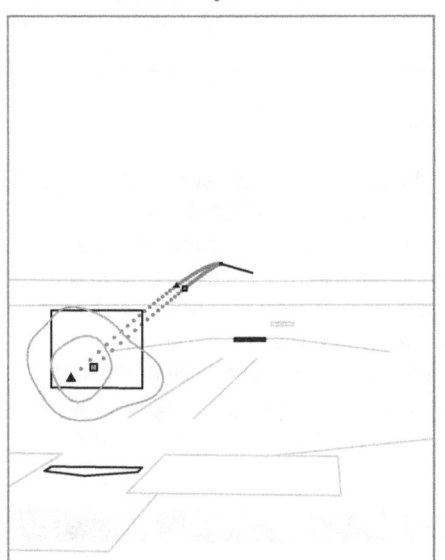	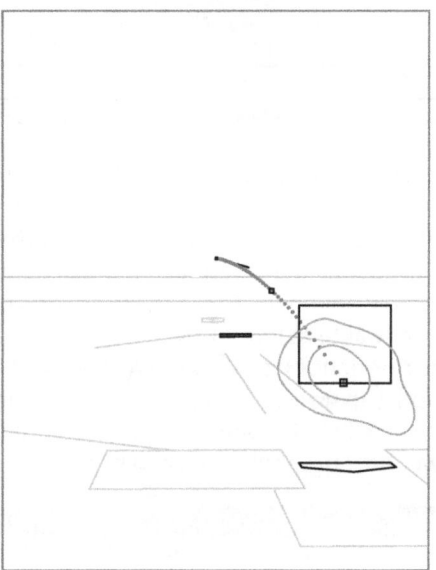

Type	Frequency	Velocity	H Movement	V Movement
● Fastball	8.5%	94.2 [105]	-6.5 [101]	-13.3 [105]
☐ Sinker	59.6%	95 [113]	-14.5 [89]	-18.3 [107]
+ Cutter	9.7%	90.5 [114]	1.1 [95]	-22.6 [106]
▲ Changeup	16.7%	88.6 [114]	-11.3 [102]	-27.1 [101]
◇ Curveball	5.5%	79.3 [102]	9.6 [108]	-46.3 [105]

Seattle Mariners 2021

Yoshihisa Hirano   RHP
Born: 03/08/84   Age: 37   Bats: R   Throws: R
Height: 6'1"   Weight: 185   Origin: International Free Agent, 2017

YEAR	TEAM	LVL	AGE	W	L	SV	G	GS	IP	H	HR	BB/9	K/9	K	GB%	BABIP
2018	ARI	MLB	34	4	3	3	75	0	66^1	49	6	3.1	8.0	59	50.6%	.251
2019	ARI	MLB	35	5	5	1	62	0	53	51	7	3.7	10.4	61	44.2%	.317
2020	SEA	MLB	36	0	1	4	13	0	12^1	18	2	5.8	8.0	11	48.8%	.390
2021 FS	*SEA*	*MLB*	*37*	*2*	*2*	*0*	*57*	*0*	*50*	*46*	*6*	*3.8*	*8.5*	*46*	*46.4%*	*.289*

Comparables: Jesse Chavez, Carlos Torres, Ricardo Rincon

The 2020 baseball season left us with a data set even a chaste Puritan would term "meager." That goes doubly so for relief pitchers, and triply for relief pitchers who missed the first half of the already-shortened season due to contracting a mysterious, new disease whose health ramifications are still largely unknown. Given these chaotic factors, it's impressive that once he was finally able to join the Mariners for the season's final month, Hirano's performance was very nearly identical to his career major-league norms. An uptick in walks and a downtick on his fastball could be a sign of age-induced decline for the soon-to-be 37-year-old, or it could be just 12 innings in the weirdest baseball season in history.

YEAR	TEAM	LVL	AGE	WHIP	ERA	DRA-	WARP	MPH	FB%	WHF	CSP
2018	ARI	MLB	34	1.09	2.44	99	0.3	93.3	53.6%	28.2%	
2019	ARI	MLB	35	1.38	4.75	93	0.4	92.7	47.9%	31.8%	
2020	SEA	MLB	36	2.11	5.84	94	0.1	91.7	45.2%	26.7%	
2021 FS	*SEA*	*MLB*	*37*	*1.36*	*4.22*	*95*	*0.4*	*92.7*	*49.1%*	*29.7%*	*41.3%*

Yoshihisa Hirano, continued

Pitch Shape vs LHH	Pitch Shape vs RHH
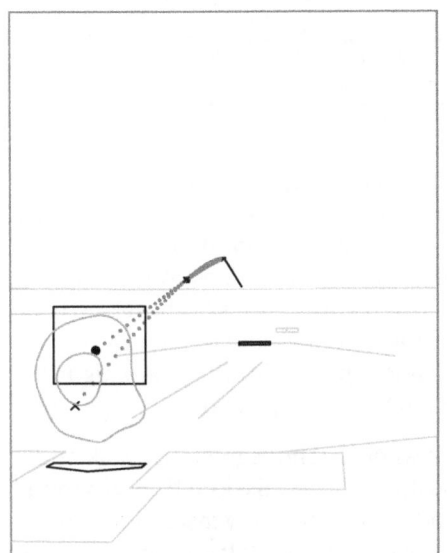	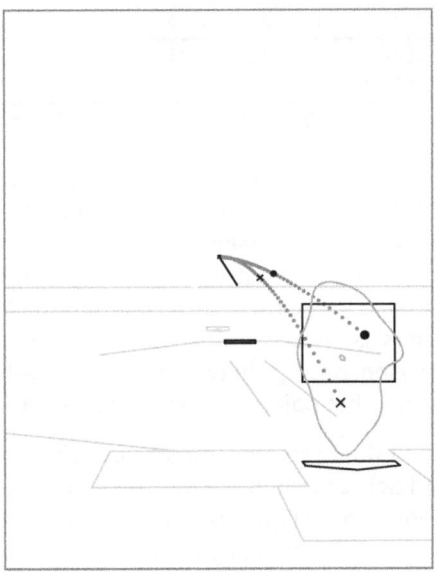

Type	Frequency	Velocity	H Movement	V Movement
● Fastball	45.2%	90 [92]	-8.7 [90]	-14.6 [102]
✕ Splitter	54.8%	82.3 [87]	-8.8 [97]	-33.8 [86]

Yusei Kikuchi   LHP

Born: 06/17/91   Age: 30   Bats: L   Throws: L
Height: 6'0"   Weight: 200   Origin: International Free Agent, 2019

YEAR	TEAM	LVL	AGE	W	L	SV	G	GS	IP	H	HR	BB/9	K/9	K	GB%	BABIP
2019	SEA	MLB	28	6	11	0	32	32	161^2	195	36	2.8	6.5	116	43.9%	.310
2020	SEA	MLB	29	2	4	0	9	9	47	41	3	3.8	9.0	47	52.8%	.306
2021 FS	SEA	MLB	30	9	8	0	26	26	150	147	21	3.5	8.1	134	46.8%	.295
2021 DC	SEA	MLB	30	8	7	0	24	24	126.3	124	18	3.5	8.1	113	46.8%	.295

Comparables: Martín Pérez, Matthew Boyd, Tyler Anderson

 We fed Kikuchi's 2020 pitching line into the MLB Player Narrative-O-Matic 3000, but it immediately began grinding horribly and spitting out acrid smoke. It shouldn't have been a surprise: The left-hander underperformed his FIP by two runs, and he did just about everything he failed to do in a disastrous 2019: limited home runs, evoked groundballs, posted above-average chase and whiff rates. By all accounts Kikuchi should have had a triumphant bounceback season, having shelved his slow curveball and replaced it with a hard, tight slider that paired well with the fastball. So where did it go wrong?

 At the beginning, mostly. Despite a lackluster (but not egregious) walk rate, Kikuchi too often put himself in a hole, posting a first strike rate that was third-worst among qualified pitchers. Command, and particularly fastball command, was never his calling card, and on 0-0 he got the pitch over the plate less often than the breaking pitch made to look like a fastball. It meant that for all his improvements, Kikuchi was routinely putting himself at a disadvantage. The silver lining to all this is that it's an easier fix than some other problems. If Kikuchi vary his tactics and reacquaint himself with strike one, we may finally see the pitcher we've long been waiting for.

YEAR	TEAM	LVL	AGE	WHIP	ERA	DRA-	WARP	MPH	FB%	WHF	CSP
2019	SEA	MLB	28	1.52	5.46	160	-3.6	94.9	49.1%	20.0%	
2020	SEA	MLB	29	1.30	5.17	83	0.8	96.6	77.4%	30.2%	
2021 FS	SEA	MLB	30	1.38	4.40	99	1.5	95.4	57.8%	23.2%	50.5%
2021 DC	SEA	MLB	30	1.38	4.40	99	1.3	95.4	57.8%	23.2%	50.5%

Yusei Kikuchi, continued

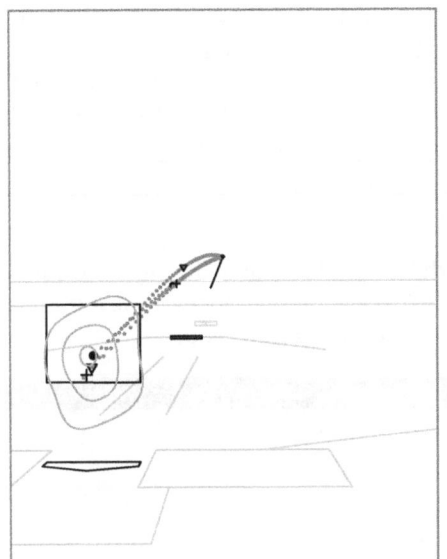
Pitch Shape vs LHH

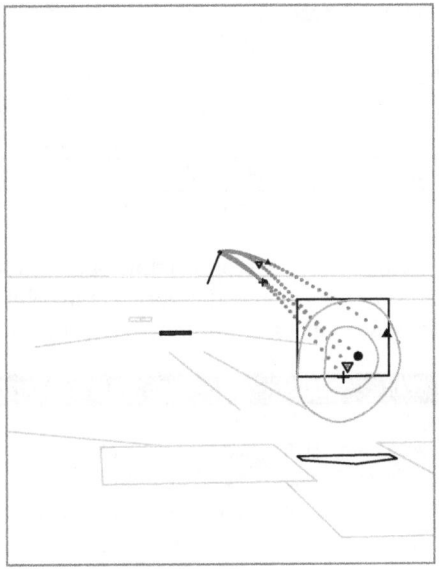
Pitch Shape vs RHH

Type	Frequency	Velocity	H Movement	V Movement
● Fastball	37.0%	95.1 [108]	5.9 [104]	-10.9 [112]
+ Cutter	39.4%	92.2 [125]	-0.9 [94]	-20.6 [114]
▲ Changeup	6.3%	86.8 [107]	9.7 [111]	-26.3 [103]
▽ Slider	16.0%	83.4 [98]	-1.3 [85]	-36.4 [92]

Brady Lail RHP

Born: 08/09/93 Age: 27 Bats: R Throws: R
Height: 6'2" Weight: 200 Origin: Round 18, 2012 Draft (#577 overall)

YEAR	TEAM	LVL	AGE	W	L	SV	G	GS	IP	H	HR	BB/9	K/9	K	GB%	BABIP
2018	TRN	AA	24	1	0	0	10	0	19¹	22	2	3.7	9.3	20	34.5%	.370
2018	SWB	AAA	24	4	6	0	27	0	43²	43	6	5.8	9.5	46	43.0%	.322
2019	TRN	AA	25	3	1	1	14	1	31	18	1	3.5	13.6	47	43.5%	.283
2019	SWB	AAA	25	1	1	0	11	0	15²	19	3	1.7	9.8	17	37.5%	.356
2019	NYY	MLB	25	0	0	0	1	0	2²	2	1	3.4	6.8	2	57.1%	.167
2020	SEA	MLB	26	0	0	0	8	0	16¹	14	5	3.9	6.6	12	32.0%	.200
2021 FS	*SEA*	*MLB*	*27*	*2*	*2*	*0*	*57*	*0*	*50*	*47*	*9*	*3.5*	*8.6*	*47*	*37.3%*	*.282*

Comparables: Chase De Jong, Joe Ross, Daniel Norris

Lail finally mastered Triple-A on his fifth try—his first came during the Obama administration—and it earned him eight 2020 relief appearances. In seven, the team was already behind; in the eighth, he coughed up the lead.

YEAR	TEAM	LVL	AGE	WHIP	ERA	DRA-	WARP	MPH	FB%	WHF	CSP
2018	TRN	AA	24	1.55	5.59	66	0.4				
2018	SWB	AAA	24	1.63	5.36	73	0.7				
2019	TRN	AA	25	0.97	1.74	56	0.7				
2019	SWB	AAA	25	1.40	7.47	100	0.2				
2019	NYY	MLB	25	1.12	10.12	123	0.0	92.9	56.5%	26.1%	
2020	SEA	MLB	26	1.29	4.41	183	-0.6	92.4	64.3%	17.1%	
2021 FS	*SEA*	*MLB*	*27*	*1.34*	*4.49*	*102*	*0.2*	*92.4*	*63.6%*	*17.9%*	*45.7%*

Brady Lail, continued

Pitch Shape vs LHH

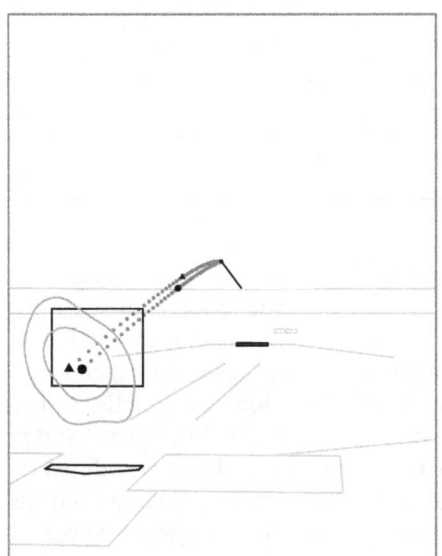

Pitch Shape vs RHH

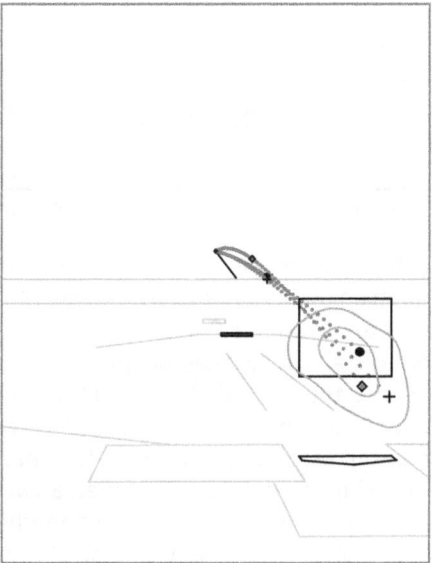

Type	Frequency	Velocity	H Movement	V Movement
● Fastball	30.3%	90.2 [92]	-4.6 [110]	-13.7 [104]
□ Sinker	18.7%	90.2 [89]	-12.8 [102]	-18.2 [108]
+ Cutter	15.3%	85.6 [83]	4.3 [115]	-25.8 [94]
▲ Changeup	16.3%	86.1 [104]	-13 [93]	-26.7 [102]
◇ Curveball	19.3%	78.9 [101]	5.5 [92]	-46.9 [103]

Nick Margevicius LHP

Born: 06/18/96   Age: 25   Bats: L   Throws: L
Height: 6'5"   Weight: 220   Origin: Round 7, 2017 Draft (#198 overall)

YEAR	TEAM	LVL	AGE	W	L	SV	G	GS	IP	H	HR	BB/9	K/9	K	GB%	BABIP
2018	FW	LO-A	22	5	5	0	13	13	76¹	79	5	1.1	10.3	87	37.0%	.349
2018	LE	HI-A	22	5	3	0	10	9	58²	69	5	1.2	9.1	59	36.0%	.379
2019	AMA	AA	23	4	4	0	12	12	69	75	14	1.7	6.9	53	42.7%	.296
2019	SD	MLB	23	2	6	0	17	12	57	73	12	3.0	6.6	42	42.7%	.332
2020	SEA	MLB	24	2	3	0	10	7	41¹	38	6	3.0	7.8	36	36.7%	.281
2021 FS	SEA	MLB	25	9	8	0	26	26	150	149	25	3.0	7.7	127	40.7%	.288
2021 DC	SEA	MLB	25	4	2	0	14	6	55.3	55	9	3.0	7.7	47	40.7%	.288

Comparables: David Peterson, Eric Lauer, Josh Fleming

    If you are a soft-tossing left-handed pitcher whose success largely hinges upon an ability to keep your fly balls from sailing over the fence, chances are Dipoto's Fabulous Fringe Factory has, at minimum, touched your career. Forced out of San Diego by actual prospects, Margevicius was a waiver wire pickup by Seattle and immediately filled the back end of the rotation with exactly the level of production you would expect for someone with an upper 80's fastball and no true out pitch. There's always the chance the secondary stuff can be refined to make him something more than a swing guy/back end starter—Marco Gonzales is proof of concept—but absent anything unexpected this is a pitcher whose 5.68 DRA represented a substantial improvement from the previous season. For now, we'll give him four out of 10 Buehrles and hope there's another 1-2 mph in the fastball to be found somewhere.

YEAR	TEAM	LVL	AGE	WHIP	ERA	DRA-	WARP	MPH	FB%	WHF	CSP
2018	FW	LO-A	22	1.15	3.07	76	1.5				
2018	LE	HI-A	22	1.31	4.30	99	0.2				
2019	AMA	AA	23	1.28	4.30	109	-0.3				
2019	SD	MLB	23	1.61	6.79	142	-0.8	90.3	54.1%	22.9%	
2020	SEA	MLB	24	1.26	4.57	117	0.0	92.2	64.2%	19.9%	
2021 FS	SEA	MLB	25	1.33	4.43	101	1.4	91.3	59.3%	21.4%	48.9%
2021 DC	SEA	MLB	25	1.33	4.43	101	0.5	91.3	59.3%	21.4%	48.9%

Nick Margevicius, continued

Pitch Shape vs LHH

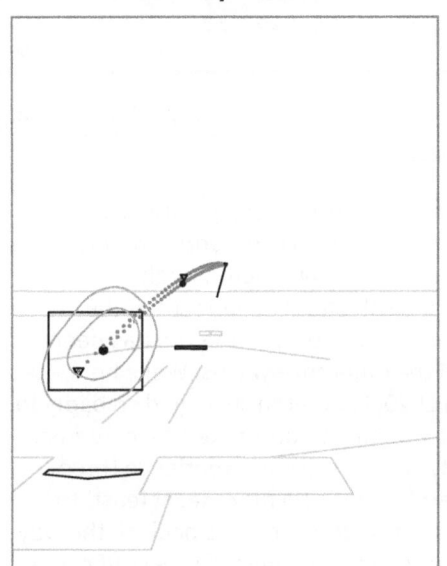

Pitch Shape vs RHH

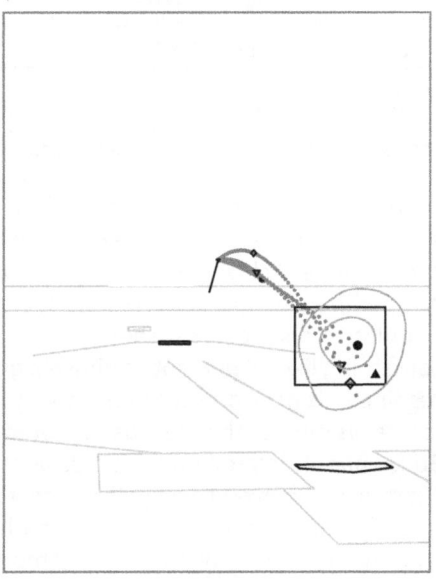

Type	Frequency	Velocity	H Movement	V Movement
● Fastball	63.7%	90.1 [92]	3.9 [113]	-14.2 [103]
▲ Changeup	8.5%	82.1 [88]	9.5 [112]	-30.1 [93]
▽ Slider	15.7%	84.3 [101]	-3.4 [93]	-30 [111]
◇ Curveball	11.3%	70.4 [68]	-8.4 [103]	-60.7 [73]

Keynan Middleton   RHP

Born: 09/12/93   Age: 27   Bats: R   Throws: R
Height: 6'3"   Weight: 215   Origin: Round 3, 2013 Draft (#95 overall)

YEAR	TEAM	LVL	AGE	W	L	SV	G	GS	IP	H	HR	BB/9	K/9	K	GB%	BABIP
2018	LAA	MLB	24	0	0	6	16	0	17²	14	1	4.6	8.2	16	33.3%	.295
2019	LAA	MLB	25	0	0	0	11	0	7²	4	0	8.2	7.0	6	35.0%	.200
2020	LAA	MLB	26	0	1	0	13	0	12	12	2	4.5	8.2	11	22.2%	.294
2021 FS	SEA	MLB	27	2	2	0	57	0	50	44	8	4.8	9.8	54	33.3%	.282
2021 DC	SEA	MLB	27	2	3	0	58	0	59.7	53	10	4.8	9.8	64	33.3%	.282

Comparables: Phil Maton, Sam Tuivailala, Edubray Ramos

    2017 seems so long ago. Remember when the US was in the Paris Climate Agreement, *The Leftovers* was still shattering hearts on HBO, and Middleton was the the Angels' closer apparent? If he watches HBO, Middleton might sympathize with *The Leftovers*' portrayal of Earth after two percent of the population disappears without a trace. Since his return, Middleton has been something like 98 percent of himself, and the difference yawns. While he regained his pre-Tommy John velocity in 2020, Middleton struggled so badly to locate his pitches that he was demoted to the Angels' alternate site in August. Still, while Middleton understands acutely what it's like to experience three years in which everything gets worse, there's reason (in his case, at least) to hope for things to improve. Pitchers whose stuff doesn't come back all the way from Tommy John surgery are common, but so are pitchers whose stuff comes back but whose precision takes longer. A surprise non-tender, the Mariners scooped him up; he'll either be the closer or in the PCL by the time the US rejoins the PCA.

YEAR	TEAM	LVL	AGE	WHIP	ERA	DRA-	WARP	MPH	FB%	WHF	CSP
2018	LAA	MLB	24	1.30	2.04	123	-0.1	98.5	64.4%	24.5%	
2019	LAA	MLB	25	1.43	1.17	107	0.0	96.4	57.3%	23.1%	
2020	LAA	MLB	26	1.50	5.25	125	-0.1	99.0	59.0%	25.0%	
2021 FS	SEA	MLB	27	1.43	4.69	103	0.2	98.3	60.0%	24.4%	47.0%
2021 DC	SEA	MLB	27	1.43	4.69	103	0.2	98.3	60.0%	24.4%	47.0%

Keynan Middleton, continued

Pitch Shape vs LHH	Pitch Shape vs RHH
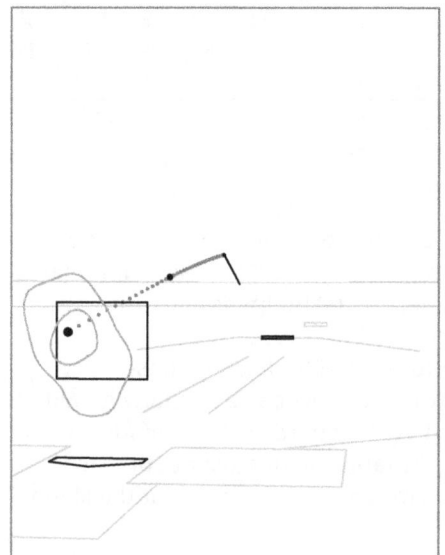	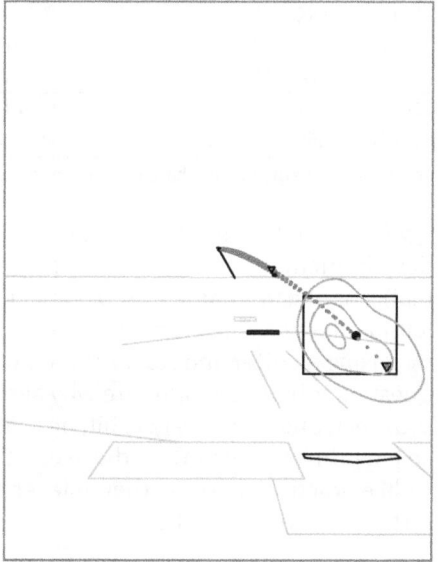

Type	Frequency	Velocity	H Movement	V Movement
● Fastball	59.0%	97.2 [115]	-7.5 [96]	-10.7 [113]
▲ Changeup	18.6%	88.3 [112]	-13.1 [92]	-24.6 [108]
▽ Slider	22.4%	87.5 [116]	2.4 [89]	-27.3 [119]

Anthony Misiewicz LHP

Born: 11/01/94 Age: 26 Bats: R Throws: L
Height: 6'1" Weight: 200 Origin: Round 18, 2015 Draft (#545 overall)

YEAR	TEAM	LVL	AGE	W	L	SV	G	GS	IP	H	HR	BB/9	K/9	K	GB%	BABIP
2018	ARK	AA	23	3	12	0	21	21	98	133	14	2.7	8.4	91	41.9%	.375
2019	ARK	AA	24	1	2	0	7	7	35^2	36	0	1.8	9.1	36	48.0%	.367
2019	TAC	AAA	24	8	6	0	19	17	95^2	95	17	2.6	8.4	89	42.8%	.292
2020	SEA	MLB	25	0	2	0	21	0	20	20	2	2.7	11.2	25	31.4%	.367
2021 FS	SEA	MLB	26	2	2	3	57	0	50	47	8	3.5	8.9	49	39.9%	.290
2021 DC	SEA	MLB	26	2	2	3	46	0	47.7	45	7	3.5	8.9	47	39.9%	.290

Comparables: Keury Mella, Chase De Jong, Andrew Moore

After bouncing along the Mallex Smith Seattle-to-Tampa Bay-to-Seattle developmental circuit, Misiewicz spent the entirety of 2020 wearing navy (and teal). For a team that featured one of the very worst bullpens in the sport, the left-hander was one of the few bright spots, setting a career-best strikeout rate by mixing a cutter and slurvy curveball with a mid-90's heater. Those questionable secondaries are why Misiewicz was never a particularly heralded prospect, and when he gets hit, he tends to get hit hard. But he's made it work so far, primarily by putting those enticing hittable pitches just out of reach. Unlike practically every other reliever that made an appearance for the Mariners last year, he figures to be back.

YEAR	TEAM	LVL	AGE	WHIP	ERA	DRA-	WARP	MPH	FB%	WHF	CSP
2018	ARK	AA	23	1.65	5.51	86	1.3				
2019	ARK	AA	24	1.21	2.52	91	0.2				
2019	TAC	AAA	24	1.29	5.36	78	2.6				
2020	SEA	MLB	25	1.30	4.05	80	0.4	94.9	76.8%	31.6%	
2021 FS	SEA	MLB	26	1.34	4.34	98	0.3	94.9	76.8%	31.6%	44.6%
2021 DC	SEA	MLB	26	1.34	4.34	98	0.3	94.9	76.8%	31.6%	44.6%

Anthony Misiewicz, continued

Pitch Shape vs LHH

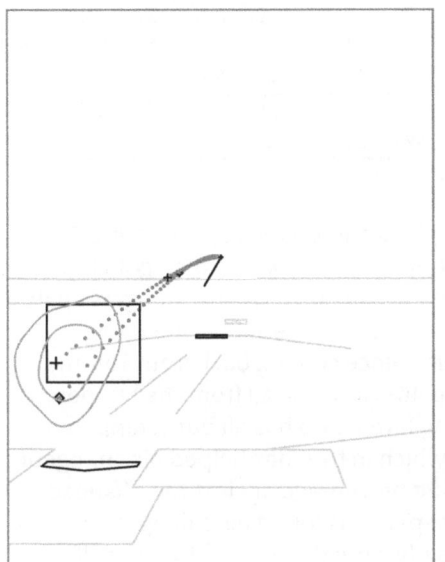

Pitch Shape vs RHH

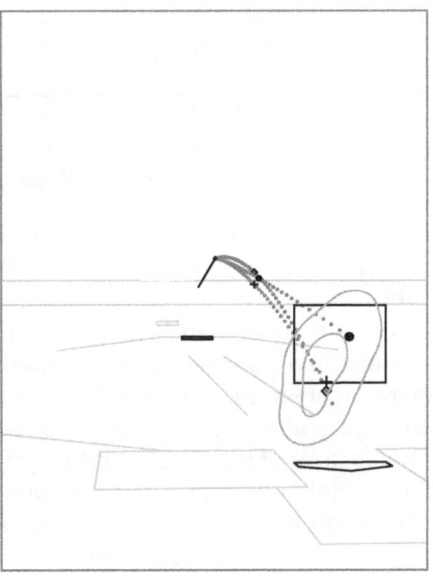

Type	Frequency	Velocity	H Movement	V Movement
● Fastball	23.9%	94.1 [105]	7.7 [95]	-13 [106]
+ Cutter	52.3%	90.1 [111]	-2.7 [105]	-22.7 [106]
◇ Curveball	23.0%	82.1 [113]	-10 [110]	-39.9 [119]

Rafael Montero RHP

Born: 10/17/90 Age: 30 Bats: R Throws: R
Height: 6'0" Weight: 190 Origin: International Free Agent, 2011

YEAR	TEAM	LVL	AGE	W	L	SV	G	GS	IP	H	HR	BB/9	K/9	K	GB%	BABIP
2019	RAN	ROK	28	0	0	0	5	3	7	2	0	0.0	15.4	12	45.5%	.182
2019	FRI	AA	28	0	0	0	5	2	9	15	0	2.0	15.0	15	25.9%	.556
2019	TEX	MLB	28	2	0	0	22	0	29	23	5	1.6	10.6	34	40.3%	.269
2020	TEX	MLB	29	0	1	8	17	0	17^2	12	2	3.1	9.7	19	26.7%	.238
2021 FS	SEA	MLB	30	2	2	23	57	0	50	44	6	3.5	10.3	57	38.3%	.295
2021 DC	SEA	MLB	30	2	2	23	58	0	59.7	52	8	3.5	10.3	68	38.3%	.295

Comparables: Kevin Gausman, Erasmo Ramírez, Chris Stratton

Don Rafael Montero jailed Anthony Hopkins and pretended Catherine Zeta-Jones was his daughter before trying to buy California with stolen gold in *The Mask of Zorro*. He saved four of his eight games in 2020 with the Rangers against teams from the Golden State, making him a much more successful Rafael Montero than his silver screen counterpart. Since coming back from Tommy John surgery in 2019, Montero has tossed 46⅔ innings, all from the bullpen, striking out almost 30 percent of opposing hitters. He has all but scrapped his slider in favor of more high-90s heaters, which in turn has helped his changeup play up, holding offenses to a .267 slugging percentage against the offspeed offering. It's fair to say the former top prospect has found his calling, and although it's not as a starter, he has certainly carved out a role for himself moving forward. He should pitch meaningful innings with the Mariners following an offseason trade.

YEAR	TEAM	LVL	AGE	WHIP	ERA	DRA-	WARP	MPH	FB%	WHF	CSP
2019	RAN	ROK	28	0.29	0.00						
2019	FRI	AA	28	1.89	7.00	128	-0.2				
2019	TEX	MLB	28	0.97	2.48	86	0.4	97.5	46.8%	29.8%	
2020	TEX	MLB	29	1.02	4.08	110	0.1	97.3	72.0%	25.0%	
2021 FS	SEA	MLB	30	1.27	3.80	87	0.6	97.4	59.0%	27.5%	46.0%
2021 DC	SEA	MLB	30	1.27	3.80	87	0.7	97.4	59.0%	27.5%	46.0%

Rafael Montero, continued

Pitch Shape vs LHH

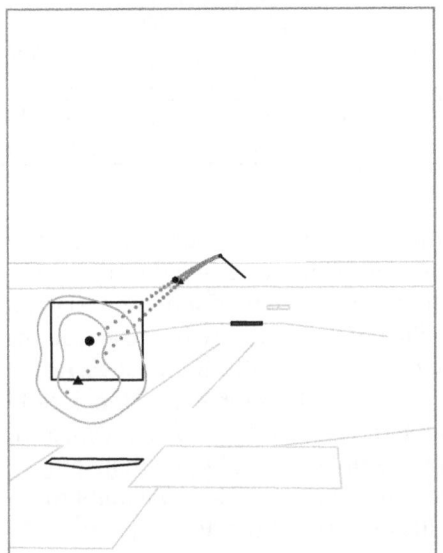

Pitch Shape vs RHH

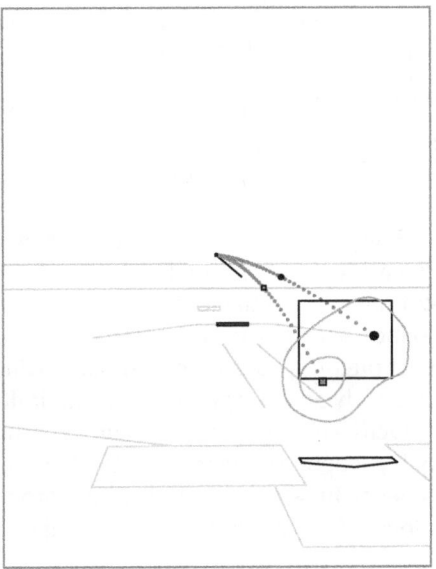

Type	Frequency	Velocity	H Movement	V Movement
● Fastball	47.8%	96 [111]	-7.7 [95]	-13.2 [106]
☐ Sinker	24.2%	94.8 [112]	-13.8 [95]	-18.7 [106]
▲ Changeup	20.8%	89.2 [116]	-13.9 [89]	-25.6 [105]
▽ Slider	7.3%	85.9 [109]	6.8 [106]	-31.3 [107]

Ljay Newsome   RHP

Born: 11/08/96   Age: 24   Bats: R   Throws: R
Height: 5'11"   Weight: 210   Origin: Round 26, 2015 Draft (#785 overall)

YEAR	TEAM	LVL	AGE	W	L	SV	G	GS	IP	H	HR	BB/9	K/9	K	GB%	BABIP
2018	MOD	HI-A	21	6	10	0	26	26	138^2	169	24	0.8	8.0	123	31.3%	.339
2019	MOD	HI-A	22	6	6	0	18	18	100^2	105	11	0.8	11.1	124	25.5%	.357
2019	ARK	AA	22	3	4	0	9	9	48^2	41	4	1.3	6.5	35	34.9%	.262
2020	SEA	MLB	23	0	1	0	5	4	15^2	20	4	0.6	5.2	9	42.1%	.302
2021 FS	SEA	MLB	24	9	8	0	26	26	150	150	26	1.7	7.4	123	38.1%	.284
2021 DC	SEA	MLB	24	2	2	0	14	6	27	27	4	1.7	7.4	22	38.1%	.284

Comparables: Tyler Mahle, Chih-Wei Hu, José Ureña

Every infomercial has that series of soundbites with overjoyed past customers swearing that PRODUCT changed their lives for the better. When the Mariners cut the infomercial for their Gas Camp, an offseason pitching summit designed to increase velocity, maximize pitch mix efficiency, and otherwise make you the best pitcher you can be, Newsome will be one of the breathless apostles. A relatively anonymous 26th-round draft pick in 2015, Newsome used increased velocity and command to skyrocket through three levels in 2019, enjoying a cup of big league coffee in 2020. While his ceiling is unlikely any higher than long reliever, his success stands as the proof of concept the Mariners will point to moving forward when evangelizing their future young pitching prospects.

YEAR	TEAM	LVL	AGE	WHIP	ERA	DRA-	WARP	MPH	FB%	WHF	CSP
2018	MOD	HI-A	21	1.31	4.87	90	1.4				
2019	MOD	HI-A	22	1.13	3.75	87	0.9				
2019	ARK	AA	22	0.99	2.77	83	0.5				
2020	SEA	MLB	23	1.34	5.17	118	0.0	93.3	49.4%	21.8%	
2021 FS	SEA	MLB	24	1.19	3.99	94	1.9	93.3	49.4%	21.8%	53.5%
2021 DC	SEA	MLB	24	1.19	3.99	94	0.3	93.3	49.4%	21.8%	53.5%

Ljay Newsome, continued

Pitch Shape vs LHH

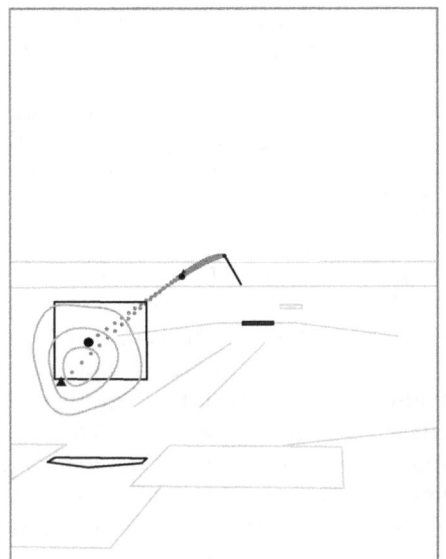

Pitch Shape vs RHH

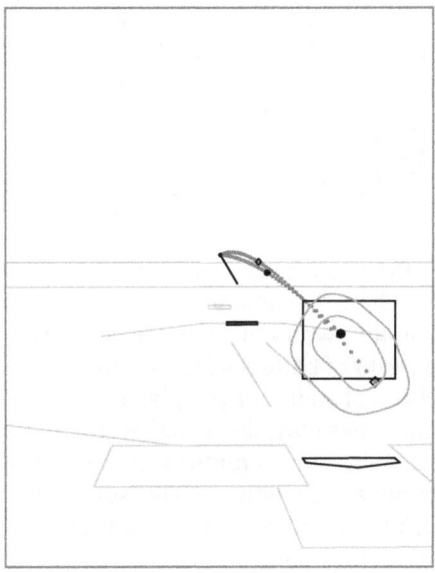

Type	Frequency	Velocity	H Movement	V Movement
● Fastball	49.4%	91.5 [97]	-7.3 [97]	-15.1 [100]
▲ Changeup	23.9%	84.7 [98]	-11.6 [101]	-31.6 [89]
◇ Curveball	26.7%	77.3 [95]	4.5 [87]	-43.1 [112]

Yohan Ramirez RHP

Born: 05/06/95 Age: 26 Bats: R Throws: R
Height: 6'4" Weight: 190 Origin: International Free Agent, 2016

YEAR	TEAM	LVL	AGE	W	L	SV	G	GS	IP	H	HR	BB/9	K/9	K	GB%	BABIP
2018	QC	LO-A	23	5	7	1	15	10	58	40	6	4.3	9.6	62	52.7%	.243
2018	FAY	HI-A	23	1	1	2	14	0	20	16	0	6.3	9.0	20	67.3%	.308
2019	FAY	HI-A	24	1	2	0	10	7	43^2	22	0	4.5	14.2	69	53.6%	.262
2019	CC	AA	24	3	5	1	17	8	62^1	42	5	7.5	12.9	89	43.4%	.285
2020	SEA	MLB	25	0	0	3	16	0	20^2	9	3	8.7	11.3	26	13.6%	.146
2021 FS	SEA	MLB	26	2	3	0	57	0	50	43	8	7.4	10.9	60	33.8%	.292
2021 DC	SEA	MLB	26	1	1	0	26	0	23.7	20	4	7.4	10.9	29	33.8%	.292

Comparables: Chad Sobotka, Wei-Chieh Huang, Tony Gonsolin

Pete Rose once said he would walk through hell in a gasoline suit to play baseball. Presumably both the gasoline and the match would be provided by Ramirez, who walked nearly as many batters as he struck out in 2020; only 48 percent of batters he faced put the ball in play. While this summary conjures the vision of another dystopian data point in nu-baseball's quest for pure three-outcomes play, the actual aesthetic experience of watching Ramirez pitch is gleefully, almost rapturously chaotic. If you ever wondered what it would be like to drive a car with a 700 horsepower engine not only lacking any safety or comfort features, but evan an ackknowledgement that safety and comfort exist as abstract concepts, this is the relief pitcher for you. He could flame out in a year or make a mechanical adjustment, harness his upper-90s fastball and wipeout slider, and become a shutdown closer. Either way, don't break glass in case of emergency, because you will quickly run out of glass.

YEAR	TEAM	LVL	AGE	WHIP	ERA	DRA-	WARP	MPH	FB%	WHF	CSP
2018	QC	LO-A	23	1.17	2.95	85	0.8				
2018	FAY	HI-A	23	1.50	3.15	71	0.4				
2019	FAY	HI-A	24	1.01	2.89	56	1.2				
2019	CC	AA	24	1.51	4.76	97	0.0				
2020	SEA	MLB	25	1.40	2.61	151	-0.4	97.1	59.8%	30.1%	
2021 FS	SEA	MLB	26	1.70	6.12	123	-0.4	97.1	59.8%	30.1%	42.6%
2021 DC	SEA	MLB	26	1.70	6.12	123	-0.2	97.1	59.8%	30.1%	42.6%

Yohan Ramirez, continued

Pitch Shape vs LHH

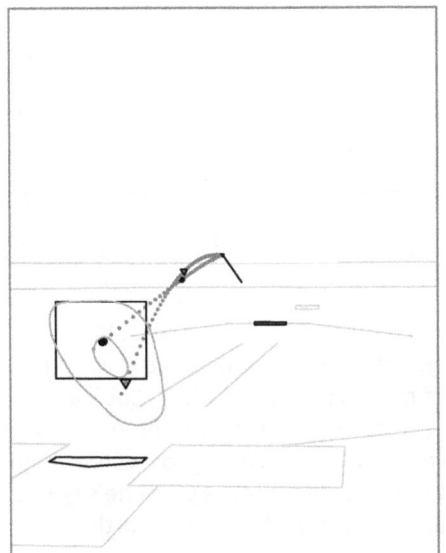

Pitch Shape vs RHH

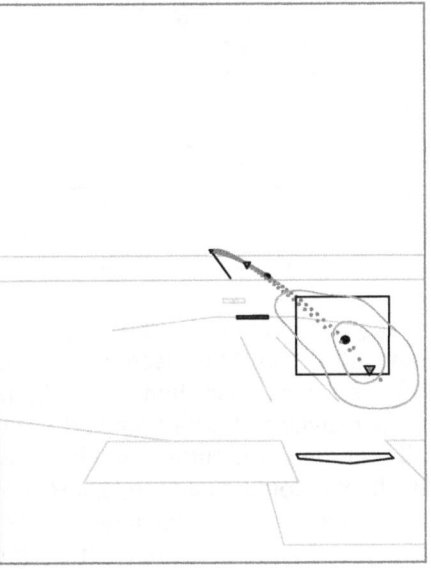

Type	Frequency	Velocity	H Movement	V Movement
● Fastball	59.0%	95.7 [110]	-8.2 [93]	-13.8 [104]
▽ Slider	39.6%	82 [91]	15.8 [140]	-33.9 [99]

Casey Sadler RHP

Born: 07/13/90 Age: 30 Bats: R Throws: R
Height: 6'3" Weight: 205 Origin: Round 25, 2010 Draft (#747 overall)

YEAR	TEAM	LVL	AGE	W	L	SV	G	GS	IP	H	HR	BB/9	K/9	K	GB%	BABIP
2018	IND	AAA	27	6	5	1	27	8	77	79	7	3.0	7.1	61	43.8%	.310
2018	PIT	MLB	27	0	0	0	2	0	4^1	9	0	6.2	6.2	3	57.9%	.474
2019	OKC	AAA	28	0	0	1	2	1	6	8	1	1.5	13.5	9	56.2%	.467
2019	DUR	AAA	28	1	1	1	11	3	32^2	30	5	1.4	12.1	44	38.8%	.312
2019	TB	MLB	28	0	0	0	9	0	19^1	16	2	2.3	5.1	11	54.8%	.233
2019	LAD	MLB	28	4	0	1	24	1	27	25	3	2.7	6.7	20	47.6%	.278
2020	SEA	MLB	29	1	2	0	17	0	19^1	15	3	5.6	9.8	21	41.5%	.245
2021 FS	SEA	MLB	30	2	2	0	57	0	50	47	7	3.3	8.4	46	46.5%	.290
2021 DC	SEA	MLB	30	2	2	0	58	0	59.7	56	8	3.3	8.4	55	46.5%	.290

Comparables: Chris Stratton, Matt Albers, Ryan Weber

Look at those numbers above, and consider that Sadler beat his 99th-percentile PECOTA projections from last year to reach them. He did it with the same stock-standard hint-of-salt 3.5-pitch mix he's always had, except leaning more heavily on his best pitch, the curve (37 percent usage) and throwing it just all over the place. Hitters couldn't restrain themselves, leading to a career-high whiff rate. Could it happen again? Sure, but if it does, at some point he's going to graduate to a leverage index above "facing Casey Sadler in the fourth inning of a game" and he may need another trick.

YEAR	TEAM	LVL	AGE	WHIP	ERA	DRA-	WARP	MPH	FB%	WHF	CSP
2018	IND	AAA	27	1.36	3.39	82	1.1				
2018	PIT	MLB	27	2.77	8.31	112	0.0	93.9	59.3%	17.1%	
2019	OKC	AAA	28	1.50	6.00	41	0.3				
2019	DUR	AAA	28	1.07	2.76	60	1.1				
2019	TB	MLB	28	1.09	1.86	110	0.0	94.9	44.3%	22.8%	
2019	LAD	MLB	28	1.22	2.33	101	0.1	95.3	34.4%	22.7%	
2020	SEA	MLB	29	1.40	5.12	84	0.3	94.2	35.6%	30.0%	
2021 FS	SEA	MLB	30	1.31	4.12	94	0.4	94.7	37.9%	25.5%	43.9%
2021 DC	SEA	MLB	30	1.31	4.12	94	0.5	94.7	37.9%	25.5%	43.9%

Casey Sadler, continued

Pitch Shape vs LHH

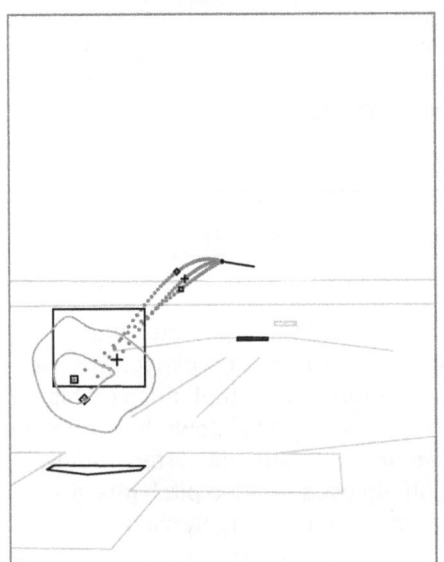

Pitch Shape vs RHH

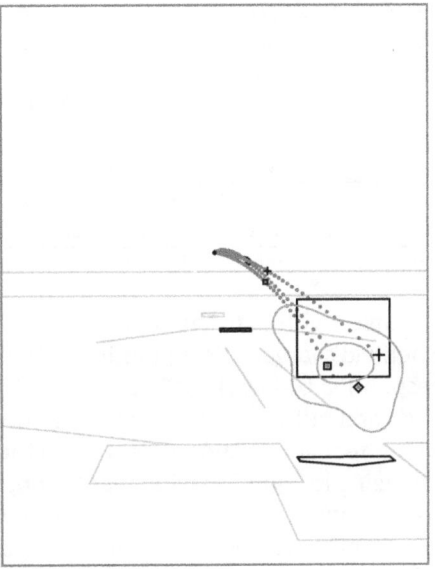

Type	Frequency	Velocity	H Movement	V Movement
☐ Sinker	35.3%	93 [103]	-14.9 [86]	-19.4 [104]
+ Cutter	23.0%	89 [104]	2.9 [106]	-24.5 [99]
▲ Changeup	4.3%	86.6 [106]	-14 [88]	-29.3 [95]
◇ Curveball	37.1%	80.7 [108]	9.6 [108]	-44.8 [108]

Justus Sheffield LHP

Born: 05/13/96   Age: 25   Bats: L   Throws: L
Height: 5'10"   Weight: 195   Origin: Round 1, 2014 Draft (#31 overall)

YEAR	TEAM	LVL	AGE	W	L	SV	G	GS	IP	H	HR	BB/9	K/9	K	GB%	BABIP
2018	TRN	AA	22	1	2	0	5	5	28	16	1	4.5	12.5	39	40.7%	.259
2018	SWB	AAA	22	6	4	0	20	15	88	66	3	3.7	8.6	84	45.9%	.264
2018	NYY	MLB	22	0	0	0	3	0	2^2	4	1	10.1	0.0	0	54.5%	.300
2019	ARK	AA	23	5	3	0	12	12	78	62	4	2.1	9.8	85	42.6%	.294
2019	TAC	AAA	23	2	6	0	13	12	55	59	12	6.7	7.9	48	53.2%	.292
2019	SEA	MLB	23	0	1	0	8	7	36	44	5	4.5	9.2	37	52.7%	.379
2020	SEA	MLB	24	4	3	0	10	10	55^1	52	2	3.3	7.8	48	49.7%	.314
2021 FS	SEA	MLB	25	9	8	0	26	26	150	146	21	4.1	8.5	142	47.9%	.299
2021 DC	SEA	MLB	25	7	7	0	25	22	117.7	115	16	4.1	8.5	111	47.9%	.299

Comparables: Yohander Méndez, Kohl Stewart, Sean Reid-Foley

Cursed with both the "twice-traded prospect" and "low spin rate" stigmas, Sheffield's largely disappointing 2019 knocked him off most prospect lists. He responded by knocking 25 percent off his walk rate, nearly that much off his DRA, and putting together a strong enough season to justify down-ballot Rookie of the Year votes. Another feather in the cap of a development system rapidly changing its industry-wide reputation, Sheffield used a varied pitch mix, a tough, biting slider, and hilariously low home run-rate to largely silence whispers that he was destined for the bullpen. While the atrophying of his once-elite stuff will most likely keep him from being anything more than a third or fourth starter in a playoff-caliber rotation, the concerns that Seattle was hilariously swindled in the James Paxton are largely allayed, at least for now.

YEAR	TEAM	LVL	AGE	WHIP	ERA	DRA-	WARP	MPH	FB%	WHF	CSP
2018	TRN	AA	22	1.07	2.25	73	0.6				
2018	SWB	AAA	22	1.16	2.56	83	1.4				
2018	NYY	MLB	22	2.62	10.12	146	-0.1	95.7	54.4%	5.3%	
2019	ARK	AA	23	1.03	2.19	77	1.1				
2019	TAC	AAA	23	1.82	6.87	102	0.9				
2019	SEA	MLB	23	1.72	5.50	119	0.0	94.6	47.8%	30.1%	
2020	SEA	MLB	24	1.30	3.58	89	0.8	93.5	48.0%	19.8%	
2021 FS	SEA	MLB	25	1.44	4.57	101	1.3	93.9	48.0%	23.0%	47.4%
2021 DC	SEA	MLB	25	1.44	4.57	101	0.9	93.9	48.0%	23.0%	47.4%

Justus Sheffield, continued

Pitch Shape vs LHH	Pitch Shape vs RHH
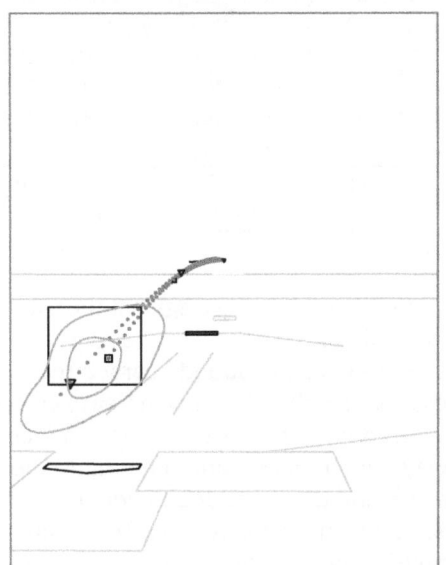	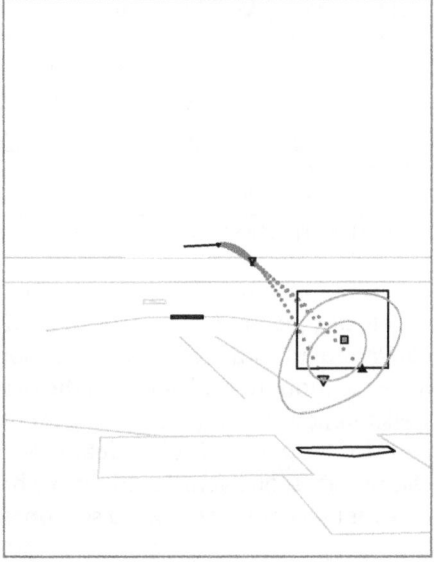

Type	Frequency	Velocity	H Movement	V Movement
☐ Sinker	47.2%	92 [98]	13.9 [94]	-22.4 [94]
▲ Changeup	18.4%	86.4 [105]	13 [93]	-31.1 [90]
▽ Slider	33.5%	81.9 [91]	-5.1 [99]	-37.7 [88]

Erik Swanson RHP

Born: 09/04/93 Age: 27 Bats: R Throws: R
Height: 6'3" Weight: 220 Origin: Round 8, 2014 Draft (#246 overall)

YEAR	TEAM	LVL	AGE	W	L	SV	G	GS	IP	H	HR	BB/9	K/9	K	GB%	BABIP
2018	SI	SS	24	0	0	0	2	2	6^2	8	0	0.0	8.1	6	47.6%	.381
2018	TRN	AA	24	5	0	0	8	7	42^2	22	0	3.2	11.6	55	34.5%	.253
2018	SWB	AAA	24	3	2	0	14	13	72^1	63	10	1.7	9.7	78	35.5%	.283
2019	TAC	AAA	25	0	1	0	10	6	24^1	28	5	4.4	10.4	28	35.2%	.348
2019	SEA	MLB	25	1	5	2	27	8	58	56	17	1.9	8.1	52	37.4%	.241
2020	SEA	MLB	26	0	2	0	9	0	7^2	11	3	2.3	10.6	9	33.3%	.381
2021 FS	SEA	MLB	27	2	2	0	57	0	50	46	9	2.7	9.0	49	36.4%	.281
2021 DC	SEA	MLB	27	1	1	0	23	0	23.7	22	4	2.7	9.0	23	36.4%	.281

Comparables: Erick Fedde, Michael Lorenzen, Drew Anderson

If ever, for some strange reason, you wanted to make a case against the value of velocity, just present Swanson's 2020 as Exhibit A. The big right-hander converted full-time to relief in the shortened-season and added nearly three miles per hour to his fastball in the process. Even with only a tiny increase in walk rate, the extra spice did almost nothing good, as his DRA soared from "very bad" to "Stop! He's already dead!" As always with relievers and their miniscule sample sizes, one year could simply be noise, and that goes double for any reliever in whatever the 2020 season was. Swanson's velocity *should* give him the ability to succeed in a major league bullpen, but first he's going to have to figure out how not only to get batter to chase, but also to get them to miss: Batters actually made contact nine percent more often on his pitches *outside* the zone than the ones *in* it.

YEAR	TEAM	LVL	AGE	WHIP	ERA	DRA-	WARP	MPH	FB%	WHF	CSP
2018	SI	SS	24	1.20	4.05	102	0.0				
2018	TRN	AA	24	0.87	0.42	75	0.9				
2018	SWB	AAA	24	1.06	3.86	75	1.5				
2019	TAC	AAA	25	1.64	5.55	114	0.2				
2019	SEA	MLB	25	1.17	5.74	121	-0.2	94.9	67.9%	22.7%	
2020	SEA	MLB	26	1.70	12.91	114	0.0	97.9	74.5%	29.6%	
2021 FS	SEA	MLB	27	1.23	4.12	96	0.4	95.5	69.1%	24.0%	49.2%
2021 DC	SEA	MLB	27	1.23	4.12	96	0.2	95.5	69.1%	24.0%	49.2%

Erik Swanson, continued

Pitch Shape vs LHH

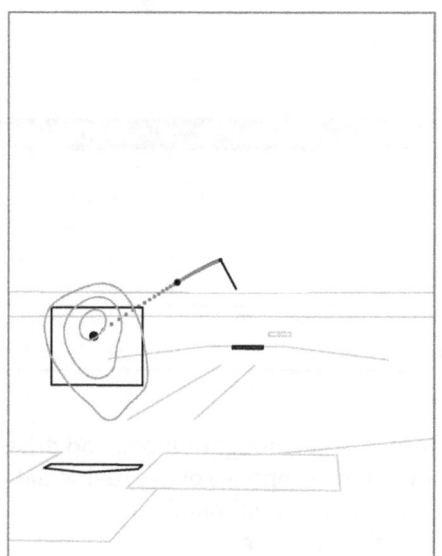

Pitch Shape vs RHH

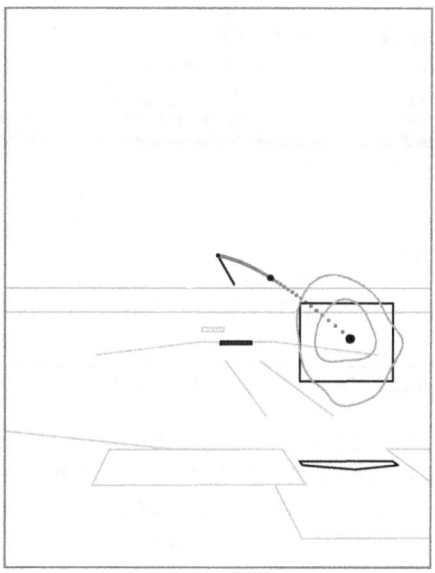

Type	Frequency	Velocity	H Movement	V Movement
● Fastball	74.5%	95.7 [110]	-8.1 [94]	-10.9 [112]
✕ Splitter	6.7%	82.7 [88]	-6.8 [104]	-31.5 [93]
▽ Slider	17.4%	88.2 [119]	4.5 [97]	-27.6 [118]

PLAYER COMMENTS WITHOUT GRAPHS

Braden Bishop CF
Born: 08/22/93   Age: 27   Bats: R   Throws: R
Height: 6'1"   Weight: 178   Origin: Round 3, 2015 Draft (#94 overall)

YEAR	TEAM	LVL	AGE	PA	R	2B	3B	HR	RBI	BB	K	SB	CS	AVG/OBP/SLG
2018	ARK	AA	24	394	70	20	0	8	33	37	68	5	2	.284/.361/.412
2019	MOD	HI-A	25	29	7	1	1	0	3	2	9	0	0	.240/.345/.360
2019	TAC	AAA	25	211	29	15	0	8	31	23	44	2	2	.276/.360/.486
2019	SEA	MLB	25	60	3	0	0	0	4	3	21	0	0	.107/.153/.107
2020	SEA	MLB	26	34	2	2	0	0	4	2	10	1	0	.167/.242/.233
2021 FS	SEA	MLB	27	600	62	24	1	12	56	46	160	2	1	.224/.297/.343
2021 DC	SEA	MLB	27	213	22	8	0	4	19	16	57	0	1	.224/.297/.343

Comparables: Harrison Bader, Xavier Paul, Kirk Nieuwenhuis

As a professional athlete, Bishop has the charisma, thoughtfulness, and drive to make a lasting positive impact in the world and potentially evoke real social change. Unfortunately, he can't hit, and performance is ultimately, tragically what determines the limits of one's signal strength.

YEAR	TEAM	LVL	AGE	PA	DRC+	BABIP	BRR	FRAA	WARP
2018	ARK	AA	24	394	139	.331	-1.9	CF(81): -0.9, RF(2): -0.1, LF(1): -0.1	1.7
2019	MOD	HI-A	25	29	55	.375	1.4	CF(3): 0.6	0.2
2019	TAC	AAA	25	211	92	.321	-0.2	CF(34): 0.7, RF(6): 1.0, LF(1): 0.0	0.6
2019	SEA	MLB	25	60	44	.171	0.2	CF(20): -0.6, LF(4): 0.2, RF(1): -0.1	-0.2
2020	SEA	MLB	26	34	84	.250	-0.4	RF(8): 0.6, CF(3): -0.3, LF(2): -0.2	0.0
2021 FS	SEA	MLB	27	600	77	.296	-0.7	CF 2, RF 1	0.3
2021 DC	SEA	MLB	27	213	77	.296	-0.2	CF 1, RF 0	0.1

Jake Fraley CF

Born: 05/25/95 Age: 26 Bats: L Throws: L
Height: 6'0" Weight: 195 Origin: Round 2, 2016 Draft (#77 overall)

YEAR	TEAM	LVL	AGE	PA	R	2B	3B	HR	RBI	BB	K	SB	CS	AVG/OBP/SLG
2018	CHA	HI-A	23	260	39	19	7	4	41	26	44	11	8	.347/.415/.547
2019	ARK	AA	24	259	40	15	2	11	47	23	55	16	5	.313/.386/.539
2019	TAC	AAA	24	168	28	12	3	8	33	11	34	6	2	.276/.333/.553
2019	SEA	MLB	24	41	3	2	0	0	1	0	14	0	0	.150/.171/.200
2020	SEA	MLB	25	29	3	1	1	0	0	2	11	2	1	.154/.241/.269
2021 FS	SEA	MLB	26	600	67	25	5	20	69	41	172	18	10	.226/.291/.406
2021 DC	SEA	MLB	26	156	17	6	1	5	18	10	44	4	3	.226/.291/.406

Comparables: Josh Kroeger, Randy Arozarena, Tyler O'Neill

The Mariners touted Fraley as a "five-tool" prospect, but never really elaborated on what those were. The mystery deepened as the team turned to seemingly every other outfielder, infielder, and sports radio host in the organization while he languished at the alternate site. Given his recent baseball performance, we assume those five tools will prove to be financial planning, cooking, personal magenetism, guitar, and Mario speed runs.

YEAR	TEAM	LVL	AGE	PA	DRC+	BABIP	BRR	FRAA	WARP
2018	CHA	HI-A	23	260	162	.407	-2.2	LF(31): 2.6, CF(21): 2.1, RF(12): 0.1	2.1
2019	ARK	AA	24	259	190	.370	-0.3	RF(21): -1.3, LF(12): -1.1, CF(12): -2.5	2.1
2019	TAC	AAA	24	168	102	.304	-1.3	CF(22): 0.9, RF(9): -0.7, LF(6): 0.5	0.5
2019	SEA	MLB	24	41	63	.231	-0.7	CF(11): -1.5, RF(1): 0.0	-0.3
2020	SEA	MLB	25	29	68	.267	0.0	RF(6): -0.1, LF(1): 0.6	0.0
2021 FS	SEA	MLB	26	600	88	.292	2.3	RF 3, LF 2	1.3
2021 DC	SEA	MLB	26	156	88	.292	0.6	RF 1, LF 0	0.3

Seattle Mariners 2021

Mitch Haniger RF
Born: 12/23/90 Age: 30 Bats: R Throws: R
Height: 6'2" Weight: 199 Origin: Round 1, 2012 Draft (#38 overall)

YEAR	TEAM	LVL	AGE	PA	R	2B	3B	HR	RBI	BB	K	SB	CS	AVG/OBP/SLG
2018	SEA	MLB	27	683	90	38	4	26	93	70	148	8	2	.285/.366/.493
2019	SEA	MLB	28	283	46	13	1	15	32	30	81	4	0	.220/.314/.463
2021 FS	SEA	MLB	30	600	84	27	2	25	72	61	157	5	2	.248/.340/.454
2021 DC	SEA	MLB	30	463	64	21	1	19	55	47	121	3	2	.248/.340/.454

Comparables: Jay Buhner, Jesse Barfield, Jay Bruce

Haniger was well on his way to becoming an established star in 2019 when a foul ball launched itself directly into his gentleman area, rupturing a testicle. What unfolded was a series of frustrating setbacks: His rehab led to a torn adductor muscle in his core, which led to a herniated disc in his back, which led to re-injuring his core, which led to re-injuring his back. Eventually they just stopped adding details.

If the skills Haniger showed from 2017-2019 remain intact—and at 30 there's a fair enough chance they are—he could return to form and be one of the American League's best right fielders. His ability to grind out at-bats, hit for power, and play quality-if-unspectacular defense forms a broad level of above-average skills, and one Seattle would be very grateful to have in its lineup. Otherwise, Mariners fans will recall another Seattle outfielder whose potential-laden career was sidelined by flukey bad luck: Franklin Gutierrez.

YEAR	TEAM	LVL	AGE	PA	DRC+	BABIP	BRR	FRAA	WARP
2018	SEA	MLB	27	683	128	.336	-3.5	RF(144): 5.0, CF(35): -2.8, LF(2): -0.2	3.9
2019	SEA	MLB	28	283	101	.257	2.0	RF(43): 3.2, CF(24): 0.4	1.4
2021 FS	SEA	MLB	30	600	116	.307	-0.4	RF 5, LF 0	3.1
2021 DC	SEA	MLB	30	463	116	.307	-0.3	RF 4	2.3

Jarred Kelenic CF
Born: 07/16/99 Age: 21 Bats: L Throws: L
Height: 6'1" Weight: 190 Origin: Round 1, 2018 Draft (#6 overall)

YEAR	TEAM	LVL	AGE	PA	R	2B	3B	HR	RBI	BB	K	SB	CS	AVG/OBP/SLG
2018	KNG	ROK	18	200	33	8	4	5	33	22	39	11	1	.253/.350/.431
2018	MTS	ROK	18	51	9	2	2	1	9	4	11	4	0	.413/.451/.609
2019	WV	LO-A	19	218	33	14	3	11	29	25	45	7	4	.309/.394/.586
2019	MOD	HI-A	19	190	36	13	1	6	22	17	49	10	3	.290/.353/.485
2019	ARK	AA	19	92	11	4	1	6	17	8	17	3	0	.253/.315/.542
2021 FS	SEA	MLB	21	600	68	24	4	20	71	39	181	10	4	.226/.282/.397
2021 DC	SEA	MLB	21	491	56	20	3	16	58	32	148	7	4	.226/.282/.397

Comparables: Oscar Taveras, Byron Buxton, Travis Snider

The Mariners franchise hasn't made the postseason since the sitcom *Friends* was at the height of its ratings power. Yes, Seattle and playoff baseball have been on quite a break. If Dipoto's rebuild is finally going to bring the two together again it's going to be because the Mets hired Robinson Canó's former agent as general manager at just the right time to be party to a potential all-time swindle.

When talking about prospects, the term "well-rounded" sometimes connotes a low-ceiling. That would be a mistake in Kelenic's case. He is indeed well-rounded, but rather than lacking any plus skills, his game simply lacks any glaring weaknesses. This is a top-10 prospect who can handle center field (at worst, capably) and put up a 134 DRC+ in Double-A at 19. That he is only *arguably* Seattle's best prospect says much more about the system's recent rise (and fellow outfield prospect Julio Rodríguez) than it does about any limits on Kelenic's future. He'll almost certainly be ready for the majors in 2021, almost just as certainly well before he makes his debut. When he does arrive, even with 2020 Rookie of the Year Kyle Lewis in the fold, there's a good chance he'll rank as Seattle's best outfielder by the time we write the 2022 Annual.

YEAR	TEAM	LVL	AGE	PA	DRC+	BABIP	BRR	FRAA	WARP
2018	KNG	ROK	18	200		.300			
2018	MTS	ROK	18	51		.514			
2019	WV	LO-A	19	218	180	.356	-0.5	CF(33): -1.8, RF(8): -0.1, LF(3): 2.3	2.3
2019	MOD	HI-A	19	190	137	.368	1.4	CF(32): 1.1, RF(8): -1.2, LF(2): -0.1	1.3
2019	ARK	AA	19	92	134	.246	0.6	CF(12): 0.6, RF(5): 0.6, LF(3): -0.2	0.7
2021 FS	SEA	MLB	21	600	82	.297	0.9	LF -1, CF 0	0.5
2021 DC	SEA	MLB	21	491	82	.297	0.7	LF -1, CF 0	0.2

Shed Long Jr. 2B

Born: 08/22/95 Age: 25 Bats: L Throws: R
Height: 5'8" Weight: 184 Origin: Round 12, 2013 Draft (#375 overall)

YEAR	TEAM	LVL	AGE	PA	R	2B	3B	HR	RBI	BB	K	SB	CS	AVG/OBP/SLG
2018	PNS	AA	22	522	75	22	5	12	56	57	123	19	6	.261/.353/.412
2019	TAC	AAA	23	250	38	7	4	9	36	20	65	1	3	.274/.335/.460
2019	SEA	MLB	23	168	21	12	1	5	15	16	40	3	3	.263/.333/.454
2020	SEA	MLB	24	128	10	5	0	3	9	11	37	4	0	.171/.242/.291
2021 FS	SEA	MLB	25	600	69	24	3	19	60	53	174	5	3	.228/.303/.392
2021 DC	SEA	MLB	25	297	34	12	1	9	29	26	86	2	2	.228/.303/.392

Comparables: Jordany Valdespin, Bret Boone, Jeff Kent

The M's Opening Day second baseman, Long was given the opportunity to be an everyday player for the first time. Injury and performance both conspired to make it an opportunity largely missed. There's no doubt that if Long is going to bounce back it will be on the strength of the power he flashed in 2019. In his encore, that power was only really used to jump on the occasional mistake, and even then he swung through many of them as his contact rates tumbled. Combine that with below-average plate discipline and questionable defense, and it's hard to visualize a scenario (barring injury) where he reclaims the starting position in Seattle. With Dylan Moore's breakout and organizational depth ever-improving, Long's road to success is now, well, not short.

YEAR	TEAM	LVL	AGE	PA	DRC+	BABIP	BRR	FRAA	WARP
2018	PNS	AA	22	522	113	.333	3.7	2B(123): -1.9	1.4
2019	TAC	AAA	23	250	75	.346	0.5	2B(21): 0.2, 3B(21): -0.9, LF(12): 0.9	0.2
2019	SEA	MLB	23	168	90	.327	0.8	2B(24): 1.0, LF(16): -0.4, 3B(1): -0.1	0.4
2020	SEA	MLB	24	128	59	.221	1.2	2B(32): -5.3, LF(1): 0.1	-0.7
2021 FS	SEA	MLB	25	600	87	.300	0.0	2B -2, 3B 0	0.6
2021 DC	SEA	MLB	25	297	87	.300	0.0	2B -1	0.3

Noelvi Marte SS

Born: 10/16/01   Age: 19   Bats: R   Throws: R
Height: 6'1"   Weight: 181   Origin: International Free Agent, 2018

YEAR	TEAM	LVL	AGE	PA	R	2B	3B	HR	RBI	BB	K	SB	CS	AVG/OBP/SLG
2019	DSL SEA	ROK	17	299	56	18	4	9	54	29	55	17	7	.309/.371/.511
2021								No projection						

It's rare for a team to hit it big on the international market in back-to-back seasons, but after Seattle scored with Julio Rodríguez they may have done it again with Marte. A big, powerful shortstop, the teenaged Dominican may end up outgrowing the position. While that would be a loss for Seattle, it's not a huge one, because the early returns on his bat are very exciting. Without a traditional stat line to scout, we're left with 300 plate appearances in 2019 in the Dominican rookie league, and close to 300 scouting reports and news stories gushing over Marte's offensive ceiling. We did finally receive one new data point by which to triangulate, as the enigmatic prospect appeared in the Arizona Fall League and acquitted himself well before positive COVID-19 tests shut it down.

YEAR	TEAM	LVL	AGE	PA	DRC+	BABIP	BRR	FRAA	WARP
2019	DSL SEA	ROK	17	299		.351			
2021					No projection				

Seattle Mariners 2021

Tom Murphy C
Born: 04/03/91   Age: 30   Bats: R   Throws: R
Height: 6'1"   Weight: 218   Origin: Round 3, 2012 Draft (#105 overall)

YEAR	TEAM	LVL	AGE	PA	R	2B	3B	HR	RBI	BB	K	SB	CS	AVG/OBP/SLG
2018	ABQ	AAA	27	264	40	16	3	17	49	22	76	4	2	.258/.333/.568
2018	COL	MLB	27	96	5	7	1	2	11	3	44	0	1	.226/.250/.387
2019	SEA	MLB	28	281	32	12	1	18	40	19	87	2	0	.273/.324/.535
2021 FS	SEA	MLB	30	600	68	22	2	25	75	40	220	2	1	.208/.270/.397
2021 DC	SEA	MLB	30	285	32	10	1	12	35	19	104	0	1	.208/.270/.397

Comparables: Kevin Brown, J.P. Arencibia, Russell Branyan

YEAR	TEAM	P. COUNT	FRM RUNS	BLK RUNS	THRW RUNS	TOT RUNS
2018	COL	2826	-0.3	0.0	0.0	-0.3
2019	SEA	9506	3.5	0.8	0.7	5.0
2021	SEA	10822	0.5	1.5	0.0	2.0
2021	SEA	10822	0.5	2.0	0.0	2.5

Murphy's stoic face and catching duties bely a combination of athleticism and strength rivaling any player on Seattle's major league roster. In 2019 he broke out and put those skills on display, improving his defense and unleashing massive dingers into the Pacific Northwest gloaming. In 2020 he broke down, as a foot injury sidelined him for the entire season. While the Mariners are very high on Cal Raleigh as the catcher of the future, there's every reason to treat Murphy as the backstop of the present, at least for 2021. If his defensive improvements from two years ago hold, he should be able to easily withstand some offensive regression. If the regression doesn't come, The Murph will be the second late-blooming catcher in as many years (after now-Padre Austin Nola) to find in Seattle the birthplace of his major league success.

YEAR	TEAM	LVL	AGE	PA	DRC+	BABIP	BRR	FRAA	WARP
2018	ABQ	AAA	27	264	109	.306	-0.9	C(52): 6.9	1.7
2018	COL	MLB	27	96	45	.404	-0.7	C(22): -0.3	-0.3
2019	SEA	MLB	28	281	105	.340	-0.9	C(67): 4.7, P(3): -0.0, LF(1): -0.0	2.0
2021 FS	SEA	MLB	30	600	78	.291	-0.4	C 5, 1B 0	1.2
2021 DC	SEA	MLB	30	285	78	.291	-0.2	C 3	0.7

Cal Raleigh C
Born: 11/26/96   Age: 24   Bats: S   Throws: R
Height: 6'3"   Weight: 215   Origin: Round 3, 2018 Draft (#90 overall)

YEAR	TEAM	LVL	AGE	PA	R	2B	3B	HR	RBI	BB	K	SB	CS	AVG/OBP/SLG
2018	EVE	SS	21	167	25	10	1	8	29	18	29	1	1	.288/.367/.534
2019	MOD	HI-A	22	348	48	19	0	22	66	33	69	4	0	.261/.336/.535
2019	ARK	AA	22	159	16	6	0	7	16	14	47	0	0	.228/.296/.414
2021 FS	SEA	MLB	24	600	73	25	1	27	79	43	174	0	1	.229/.289/.429
2021 DC	SEA	MLB	24	32	3	1	0	1	4	2	9	0	0	.229/.289/.429

Comparables: Jason Castro, Yasmani Grandal, Max Ramirez

Big-bodied catchers call to mind Dr. Tobais Funke's thoughts on open marriages: "Everyone deludes themselves into thinking it will work, but it never does. But...it might for us." Raleigh's future behind the dish will continue to be closely tied to how well he hits, which thus far in his career he has done very well. His defense, at least for now, seems unlikely to embarrass; his glove work is solid and footwork generally acceptable. If he hits well for a catcher, which, granted, requires maybe two extra-base hits a week these days, his path to Seattle seems clear. If he hits *really* well for a catcher, Seattle is going to have to figure out a way to limit his wear and tear behind the dish to protect his bat. If he hits just okay for a catcher, well, the calculus becomes a lot simpler, but in a way neither Raleigh or Seattle would prefer.

YEAR	TEAM	P. COUNT	FRM RUNS	BLK RUNS	THRW RUNS	TOT RUNS
2019	ARK	3371	1.0	0.0	-1.4	-0.4
2021	SEA	1202	0.1	-0.1	0.0	0.0
2021	SEA	1202	0.1	-0.3	0.0	-0.3

YEAR	TEAM	LVL	AGE	PA	DRC+	BABIP	BRR	FRAA	WARP
2018	EVE	SS	21	167	140	.309	0.3	C(25): -0.2	0.7
2019	MOD	HI-A	22	348	150	.267	0.8	C(55): 0.9	3.1
2019	ARK	AA	22	159	108	.286	-0.6	C(26): -0.0	0.6
2021 FS	SEA	MLB	24	600	93	.282	-0.9	C -3	1.5
2021 DC	SEA	MLB	24	32	93	.282	0.0	C 0	0.1

Joe Rizzo 3B
Born: 03/31/98 Age: 23 Bats: L Throws: R
Height: 5'10" Weight: 194 Origin: Round 2, 2016 Draft (#50 overall)

YEAR	TEAM	LVL	AGE	PA	R	2B	3B	HR	RBI	BB	K	SB	CS	AVG/OBP/SLG
2018	MOD	HI-A	20	508	46	21	2	4	55	40	108	6	1	.241/.303/.321
2019	MOD	HI-A	21	570	77	30	3	10	63	45	94	0	3	.295/.354/.423
2021 FS	SEA	MLB	23	600	52	23	1	10	55	42	175	0	1	.221/.280/.330

Comparables: Ryan Wheeler, Jeimer Candelario, Brandon Laird

Rizzo managed to get his slugging a tick over .400 after repeating the Cal league. He'll need to buff his bat-to-ball skills to a Lyle Overbay-level sheen and/or find a magic lamp and wish for Evan White-grade defensive skills in order to progress into the upper minors in 2021. The M's felt comfortable enough in his lamplessness to leave him unprotected in the Rule 5 draft.

YEAR	TEAM	LVL	AGE	PA	DRC+	BABIP	BRR	FRAA	WARP
2018	MOD	HI-A	20	508	77	.303	-0.9	3B(99): 0.5, 2B(6): -0.1, 1B(5): -0.3	-1.0
2019	MOD	HI-A	21	570	131	.343	4.0	3B(85): -2.3, 1B(31): -2.1, 2B(8): -0.5	3.0
2021 FS	SEA	MLB	23	600	66	.303	-0.9	3B -1, 1B -1	-1.8

Julio Y. Rodriguez OF

Born: 12/29/00 Age: 20 Bats: R Throws: R
Height: 6'3" Weight: 180 Origin: International Free Agent, 2017

YEAR	TEAM	LVL	AGE	PA	R	2B	3B	HR	RBI	BB	K	SB	CS	AVG/OBP/SLG
2018	DSL SEA	ROK	17	255	50	13	9	5	36	30	40	10	0	.315/.404/.525
2019	WV	LO-A	18	295	50	20	1	10	50	20	65	1	3	.293/.359/.490
2019	MOD	HI-A	18	72	13	6	3	2	19	5	10	0	0	.462/.514/.738
2021 FS	SEA	MLB	20	600	53	23	4	12	58	35	177	3	1	.224/.278/.351

Comparables: Bryce Harper, Jason Heyward, Chris Marrero

Every big idea needs a wow factor, and for Seattle's rebuild, it's Rodriguez. Featuring one of the elite hit tools in the minor leagues, he has never failed to destroy the pitching at every level he has faced. The big right-hander's bat control, plate discipline, and above-average athleticism give his offense arguably as high a ceiling as any prospect in the game. While nagging injuries have cost him some development time, and his large frame may see him moved off his current corner outfield spot sooner rather than later, he's still going to be just 20 years old for all of 2021. Even a median outcome for his offensive development should produce a quality young bat, and if he reaches his full potential Seattle will have one of the great offensive forces in the sport for years to come. With an exuberant, outgoing personality Rodriguez has become the defacto poster child for Dipoto's Great AL West Conquest (departure date: TBD) for a team desparate to make the playoffs for just the second time since Rodriguez has been alive.

YEAR	TEAM	LVL	AGE	PA	DRC+	BABIP	BRR	FRAA	WARP
2018	DSL SEA	ROK	17	255		.364			
2019	WV	LO-A	18	295	159	.351	0.0	RF(40): 4.7, CF(22): -0.2	2.8
2019	MOD	HI-A	18	72	254	.528	0.5	CF(13): -3.4, RF(3): -0.5	0.9
2021 FS	SEA	MLB	20	600	73	.305	0.1	RF 8, CF -1	0.0

Taylor Trammell CF

Born: 09/13/97   Age: 23   Bats: L   Throws: L
Height: 6'2"   Weight: 213   Origin: Round 1, 2016 Draft (#35 overall)

YEAR	TEAM	LVL	AGE	PA	R	2B	3B	HR	RBI	BB	K	SB	CS	AVG/OBP/SLG
2018	DAY	HI-A	20	461	71	19	4	8	41	58	105	25	10	.277/.375/.406
2019	CHA	AA	21	381	47	8	3	6	33	54	86	17	4	.236/.349/.336
2019	AMA	AA	21	133	14	4	1	4	10	13	36	3	4	.229/.316/.381
2021 FS	SEA	MLB	23	600	58	23	4	14	61	57	185	17	7	.223/.302/.362

Comparables: Ryan Kalish, Michael Saunders, Brandon Nimmo

If there were ever a prospect to make you sigh in relief that the old scouts vs. stats wars are over, it's Trammell. In the Ancient Times, a.k.a. 2012, stat guys would sit you down and Clockwork Orange your eyes open while they harangued you about how Trammell's route efficiency makes him a suspect center fielder. Scouts would cue up Futures Games highlights, show you hand-clocked home-to-first times, and ask you if you'd seen *Trouble With the Curve*. It's good that both sides have learned to appreciate what the other has to offer. Rather than argue over what Trammell is or isn't we can be brief: He's a fabulously athletic player with 70-grade speed, enough power to hit 30 home runs in a season, and enough contact and route-running issues to worry if either will ever translate to the major leagues. If it all pans out Trammell will be one of the best and most exciting outfielders in the league, but he'll have to show he can hit consistently in a way that, up until now, he simply has not.

YEAR	TEAM	LVL	AGE	PA	DRC+	BABIP	BRR	FRAA	WARP
2018	DAY	HI-A	20	461	125	.358	-0.8	CF(60): -1.7, LF(29): 4.5, RF(14): -0.7	1.7
2019	CHA	AA	21	381	110	.299	2.1	LF(91): -0.7, CF(1): 0.1	1.5
2019	AMA	AA	21	133	89	.295	-0.6	CF(31): -1.4	0.1
2021 FS	SEA	MLB	23	600	82	.312	1.6	LF 4, CF 2	1.2

Donovan Walton 2B

Born: 05/25/94   Age: 27   Bats: L   Throws: R
Height: 5'10"   Weight: 175   Origin: Round 5, 2016 Draft (#147 overall)

YEAR	TEAM	LVL	AGE	PA	R	2B	3B	HR	RBI	BB	K	SB	CS	AVG/OBP/SLG
2018	MOD	HI-A	24	256	35	12	3	3	19	30	37	8	3	.309/.402/.433
2018	ARK	AA	24	238	22	14	1	1	22	21	34	3	1	.236/.325/.327
2019	ARK	AA	25	558	72	22	3	11	50	63	72	10	13	.300/.390/.427
2019	SEA	MLB	25	19	2	0	0	0	2	3	5	0	1	.188/.316/.188
2020	SEA	MLB	26	14	0	1	0	0	3	1	5	0	1	.154/.214/.231
2021 FS	SEA	MLB	27	600	66	23	2	14	59	51	137	3	3	.234/.309/.369
2021 DC	SEA	MLB	27	30	3	1	0	0	2	2	6	0	0	.234/.309/.369

Comparables: Gavin Cecchini, Vimael Machín, Steve Tolleson

A Bloomquist by any other name, Walton will spend 2021 as he spends all years: fulfilling the words of the Good Book. "Wherever two or more are in need of grit, Donovan is with thee."

YEAR	TEAM	LVL	AGE	PA	DRC+	BABIP	BRR	FRAA	WARP
2018	MOD	HI-A	24	256	148	.358	-0.3	2B(36): -4.2, SS(19): 1.0	1.1
2018	ARK	AA	24	238	83	.276	-1.4	2B(62): 6.2	0.2
2019	ARK	AA	25	558	159	.333	-2.0	SS(103): 12.4, 2B(19): 1.6	6.6
2019	SEA	MLB	25	19	82	.273	-0.2	SS(5): -0.7, 2B(2): -0.5	-0.1
2020	SEA	MLB	26	14	85	.250		SS(4): 0.0, 2B(1): -0.0	0.0
2021 FS	SEA	MLB	27	600	86	.287	-0.4	SS 3, 2B 0	1.0
2021 DC	SEA	MLB	27	30	86	.287	0.0	SS 0	0.1

Brandon Brennan   RHP
Born: 07/26/91   Age: 29   Bats: R   Throws: R
Height: 6'4"   Weight: 207   Origin: Round 4, 2012 Draft (#141 overall)

YEAR	TEAM	LVL	AGE	W	L	SV	G	GS	IP	H	HR	BB/9	K/9	K	GB%	BABIP
2018	BIR	AA	26	4	3	1	40	1	69^2	54	4	2.7	9.0	70	52.1%	.267
2018	CHA	AAA	26	1	1	0	4	0	5	3	0	5.4	16.2	9	75.0%	.375
2019	TAC	AAA	27	1	0	0	9	0	8^2	5	1	4.2	10.4	10	82.4%	.250
2019	SEA	MLB	27	3	6	0	44	0	47^1	34	6	4.6	8.9	47	54.4%	.235
2020	SEA	MLB	28	0	0	0	5	0	7^1	7	2	6.1	8.6	7	38.1%	.263
2021 FS	SEA	MLB	29	2	2	0	57	0	50	44	6	4.9	9.3	51	49.1%	.289
2021 DC	SEA	MLB	29	2	2	0	46	0	47.7	42	6	4.9	9.3	49	49.1%	.289

Comparables: Hansel Robles, Dominic Leone, Kyle Finnegan

You've already been warned to take 2020 stats with a grain of salt, but in Brennan's case, what work you see was marred by the recovery of a strained oblique that erased most of his short season. Of course, you also have perfectly good 2019 numbers that say the same thing: The former Rule 5 pick can't throw his breaking pitches for strikes, and shouldn't throw his four-seam at all. This is not an ideal combination for a pitcher.

YEAR	TEAM	LVL	AGE	WHIP	ERA	DRA-	WARP	MPH	FB%	WHF	CSP
2018	BIR	AA	26	1.08	3.10	53	2.0				
2018	CHA	AAA	26	1.20	5.40	25	0.2				
2019	TAC	AAA	27	1.04	1.04	55	0.3				
2019	SEA	MLB	27	1.23	4.56	73	0.9	96.3	51.5%	34.4%	
2020	SEA	MLB	28	1.64	3.68	109	0.0	94.8	51.3%	32.7%	
2021 FS	SEA	MLB	29	1.44	4.37	97	0.3	96.0	51.5%	34.1%	43.4%
2021 DC	SEA	MLB	29	1.44	4.37	97	0.3	96.0	51.5%	34.1%	43.4%

Sam Carlson   RHP
Born: 12/03/98   Age: 22   Bats: R   Throws: R
Height: 6'4"   Weight: 195   Origin: Round 2, 2017 Draft (#55 overall)

Despite throwing only three professional innings since being drafted in 2017, the once highly touted Carlson is still just 22. People that age aren't supposed to have it all figured out anyway, so he's right on schedule.

Seattle Mariners 2021

Sam Delaplane   RHP
Born: 03/27/95   Age: 26   Bats: R   Throws: R
Height: 5'11"   Weight: 175   Origin: Round 23, 2017 Draft (#693 overall)

YEAR	TEAM	LVL	AGE	W	L	SV	G	GS	IP	H	HR	BB/9	K/9	K	GB%	BABIP
2018	CLI	LO-A	23	4	2	10	39	0	59^2	54	5	3.3	15.1	100	49.3%	.386
2019	MOD	HI-A	24	3	2	2	21	0	31^2	22	2	4.0	17.6	62	36.0%	.417
2019	ARK	AA	24	3	1	5	25	0	37	13	2	2.2	14.1	58	35.9%	.180
2021 FS	SEA	MLB	26	2	2	0	57	0	50	39	7	4.0	12.5	69	39.3%	.291
2021 DC	SEA	MLB	26	1	1	0	29	0	29.7	23	4	4.0	12.5	41	39.3%	.291

Comparables: Bryan Garcia, Kodi Whitley, Tyler Rogers

A 23rd-round pick in 2017, Delaplane is easily Seattle's best relief prospect. His motion is a tight coil, leg half raised, torquing his body from the right edge of the rubber toward the center of the mound. It's a very satisfying delivery, especially, as in an act of foreshadowing, he punches the ball into his glove in the windup, a precursor to a slider evading the bat and striking the catcher's mitt. That slider is a major weapon: Gripped like a curveball and thrown with the twist of a doorknob, it's heavier than the average breaking ball, which accounts for the impressive strikeout totals. He belongs in the M's bullpen on Opening Day.

YEAR	TEAM	LVL	AGE	WHIP	ERA	DRA-	WARP	MPH	FB%	WHF	CSP
2018	CLI	LO-A	23	1.27	1.96	39	2.1				
2019	MOD	HI-A	24	1.14	4.26	62	0.6				
2019	ARK	AA	24	0.59	0.49	32	1.4				
2021 FS	SEA	MLB	26	1.23	3.61	85	0.6				
2021 DC	SEA	MLB	26	1.23	3.61	85	0.4				

Roenis Elías   LHP
Born: 08/01/88   Age: 32   Bats: L   Throws: L
Height: 6'1"   Weight: 205   Origin: International Free Agent, 2011

YEAR	TEAM	LVL	AGE	W	L	SV	G	GS	IP	H	HR	BB/9	K/9	K	GB%	BABIP
2018	TAC	AAA	29	2	4	0	10	7	33^2	32	1	4.0	8.3	31	43.0%	.316
2018	WOR	AAA	29	1	0	1	4	0	7^1	2	1	2.5	11.0	9	46.7%	.071
2018	SEA	MLB	29	3	1	0	23	4	51	46	1	2.8	6.0	34	34.6%	.285
2019	SEA	MLB	30	4	2	14	44	0	47	41	8	3.3	8.6	45	35.0%	.252
2019	WAS	MLB	30	0	0	0	4	0	3	5	2	3.0	6.0	2	30.0%	.375
2021 FS	SEA	MLB	32	2	3	0	57	0	50	51	9	3.7	8.0	44	37.1%	.294

Comparables: Anthony DeSclafani, Erasmo Ramírez, Chad Bettis

Elias has pitched all of three innings since the Nationals got him at the 2019 trade deadline, including time missed this year with forearm pain, potentially undoing what had looked like a career-saving conversion to relief.

YEAR	TEAM	LVL	AGE	WHIP	ERA	DRA-	WARP	MPH	FB%	WHF	CSP
2018	TAC	AAA	29	1.40	4.54	94	0.4				
2018	WOR	AAA	29	0.55	1.23	60	0.2				
2018	SEA	MLB	29	1.22	2.65	119	-0.2	95.7	54.9%	20.7%	
2019	SEA	MLB	30	1.23	3.64	102	0.2	95.5	57.3%	26.9%	
2019	WAS	MLB	30	2.00	9.00	258	-0.2	95.7	60.0%	20.0%	
2021 FS	SEA	MLB	32	1.44	5.22	114	-0.2	95.6	56.6%	24.5%	49.8%

Aaron Fletcher LHP

Born: 02/25/96   Age: 25   Bats: L   Throws: L
Height: 6'0"   Weight: 220   Origin: Round 14, 2018 Draft (#431 overall)

YEAR	TEAM	LVL	AGE	W	L	SV	G	GS	IP	H	HR	BB/9	K/9	K	GB%	BABIP
2018	NAT	ROK	22	0	0	0	1	0	2	4	0	4.5	9.0	2	50.0%	.667
2018	AUB	SS	22	2	1	0	12	7	29	30	0	0.9	9.9	32	61.0%	.366
2019	HAG	LO-A	23	2	3	1	15	0	28	14	0	1.6	9.0	28	41.7%	.200
2019	FBG	HI-A	23	3	1	0	12	0	26	15	1	2.8	11.1	32	54.2%	.241
2019	ARK	AA	23	0	0	0	9	0	13	14	0	2.1	10.4	15	55.6%	.389
2019	HBG	AA	23	0	0	0	5	0	6¹	7	0	2.8	12.8	9	62.5%	.438
2020	SEA	MLB	24	0	0	0	6	0	4¹	7	1	14.5	14.5	7	46.2%	.500
2021 FS	SEA	MLB	25	2	2	0	57	0	50	47	7	3.8	8.7	48	46.4%	.293
2021 DC	SEA	MLB	25	0	0	0	11	0	11.7	11	1	3.8	8.7	11	46.4%	.293

Comparables: Alex Vesia, Phillip Diehl, Alex Reyes

Fletcher made his major league debut in 2020 against all odds and a good amount of reason. In celebration, we offer a glint of optimism: All the Fletchers in baseball history, dating all the way back to Sam "Bats Unknown" Fletcher in 1909, have combined for a 6.45 ERA on a mere 47 2/3 innings. In terms of the latter, Aaron is already nearly a tenth of the way there. In fact, he's already surpassed the median Fletcher in career strikeouts. So don't think of his 2020 line as a failure; think of it as taking part in a proud tradition.

YEAR	TEAM	LVL	AGE	WHIP	ERA	DRA-	WARP	MPH	FB%	WHF	CSP
2018	NAT	ROK	22	2.50	9.00						
2018	AUB	SS	22	1.14	2.48	237	-2.0				
2019	HAG	LO-A	23	0.68	1.61	50	0.8				
2019	FBG	HI-A	23	0.88	1.38	58	0.6				
2019	ARK	AA	23	1.31	3.46	114	-0.2				
2019	HBG	AA	23	1.42	4.26	96	0.0				
2020	SEA	MLB	24	3.23	12.46	96	0.0	94.5	65.3%	26.3%	
2021 FS	SEA	MLB	25	1.38	4.51	101	0.2	94.5	65.3%	26.3%	40.0%
2021 DC	SEA	MLB	25	1.38	4.51	101	0.0	94.5	65.3%	26.3%	40.0%

Seattle Mariners 2021

Chris Flexen RHP
Born: 07/01/94 Age: 27 Bats: R Throws: R
Height: 6'3" Weight: 250 Origin: Round 14, 2012 Draft (#440 overall)

YEAR	TEAM	LVL	AGE	W	L	SV	G	GS	IP	H	HR	BB/9	K/9	K	GB%	BABIP
2018	LV	AAA	23	6	7	0	18	17	92	109	11	3.0	7.6	78	41.3%	.356
2018	NYM	MLB	23	0	2	0	4	1	6^1	14	2	8.5	4.3	3	40.0%	.429
2019	SYR	AAA	24	5	3	0	26	14	78^2	94	11	2.4	10.5	92	43.9%	.382
2019	NYM	MLB	24	0	3	0	9	1	13^2	15	1	8.6	6.6	10	34.0%	.304
2021 FS	SEA	MLB	26	9	8	0	26	26	150	144	25	3.8	8.2	136	41.0%	.284
2021 DC	SEA	MLB	26	6	6	0	19	19	97	93	16	3.8	8.2	88	41.0%	.284

Comparables: Keury Mella, Lucas Sims, Jayson Aquino

Flexen's dominant finish to the season—three runs and 42 strikeouts in 31 October innings, followed by 38 punchouts and a 1.91 ERA in 28 postseason frames—underscored what we knew all along: On talent, he had little reason to spend his age-25 season in South Korea. A million dollars and a chance to escape the Wilpons' domain would tempt any young fellow, though, and so off he went to Doosan. Flexen's gamble paid off handsomely, as a strong season in the KBO undoubtedly aided his long-term MLB prospects more than anything else he could have done in 2020. His gas was a good five ticks faster than the average KBO heater, and when he located his slider effectively, he was practically unhittable; his highlight reel features some of the season's most embarrassing and half-hearted swings-and-misses. The only flaw in his game at this point is injuries: Even after missing 10 starts, 140 innings was a career high, a total that provided an advantage against the limited workloads of other free agents. He signed a two-year contract with the Seattle Mariners, and will compete for a spot in their six-man rotation in 2021.

YEAR	TEAM	LVL	AGE	WHIP	ERA	DRA-	WARP	MPH	FB%	WHF	CSP
2018	LV	AAA	23	1.52	4.40	109	0.5				
2018	NYM	MLB	23	3.16	12.79	166	-0.2	94.3	62.3%	14.1%	
2019	SYR	AAA	24	1.46	4.46	109	1.0				
2019	NYM	MLB	24	2.05	6.59	123	-0.1	96.8	61.7%	20.4%	
2021 FS	SEA	MLB	26	1.38	4.59	103	1.2	96.2	61.8%	19.0%	46.7%
2021 DC	SEA	MLB	26	1.38	4.59	103	0.6	96.2	61.8%	19.0%	46.7%

Logan Gilbert RHP
Born: 05/05/97   Age: 24   Bats: R   Throws: R
Height: 6'6"   Weight: 225   Origin: Round 1, 2018 Draft (#14 overall)

YEAR	TEAM	LVL	AGE	W	L	SV	G	GS	IP	H	HR	BB/9	K/9	K	GB%	BABIP
2019	WV	LO-A	22	1	0	0	5	5	22^2	9	2	2.4	14.3	36	22.5%	.184
2019	MOD	HI-A	22	5	3	0	12	12	62^1	52	3	1.7	10.5	73	45.5%	.322
2019	ARK	AA	22	4	2	0	9	9	50	34	2	2.7	10.1	56	32.5%	.274
2021 FS	SEA	MLB	24	2	2	0	57	0	50	43	7	3.6	9.6	53	34.5%	.282
2021 DC	SEA	MLB	24	3	2	0	6	9	45.7	40	6	3.6	9.6	48	34.5%	.282

Comparables: Jordan Yamamoto, David Price, Sean Nolin

A first-round pick in 2018, Gilbert was an advanced college arm drafted to ascend rapidly and reinforce a Seattle rotation in desperate need of power pitching. Perhaps fortunately for the young right-hander, the 2019 season happened, and suddenly the organization was a lot less desperate. His classic four-pitch arsenal maxes out with a plus curveball with big, sharp, one-to-seven movement, complemented by an above average fastball and slider. The changeup still needs work, but even with it as a show-me offering Gilbert profiles as the best drafted/developed arm of the Dipoto Regime. He should be ready for major-league action as soon as, the "timing" works out in 2021.

YEAR	TEAM	LVL	AGE	WHIP	ERA	DRA-	WARP	MPH	FB%	WHF	CSP
2019	WV	LO-A	22	0.66	1.59	31	1.0				
2019	MOD	HI-A	22	1.03	1.73	65	1.4				
2019	ARK	AA	22	0.98	2.88	73	0.8				
2021 FS	SEA	MLB	24	1.28	4.01	94	0.4				
2021 DC	SEA	MLB	24	1.28	4.01	94	0.6				

Emerson Hancock RHP
Born: 05/31/99   Age: 22   Bats: R   Throws: R
Height: 6'4"   Weight: 213   Origin: Round 1, 2020 Draft (#6 overall)

Everyone has a type, and Jerry Dipoto's is college pitchers. As the sixth-overall pick of the 2020 draft, Hancock joins George Kirby, Logan Gilbert, Isaiah Campbell, and other recent draftees in Seattle. The Georgia product features a classic power arsenal, with a fastball touching 99, and a hard, mid-80s slider. He'll need to improve his comfort with his changeup, largely because hitters in the SEC didn't really need to see a changeup to struggle with a 99 mph fastball. If Hancock reaches his potential, he's an upper-rotation arm for the 2023 Mariners. Regardless, he's another arrow in a Seattle quiver that is now bristling with talented young arms, increasing the odds a few of them hit the target.

Seattle Mariners 2021

George Kirby RHP
Born: 02/04/98 Age: 23 Bats: R Throws: R
Height: 6'4" Weight: 215 Origin: Round 1, 2019 Draft (#20 overall)

YEAR	TEAM	LVL	AGE	W	L	SV	G	GS	IP	H	HR	BB/9	K/9	K	GB%	BABIP
2019	EVE	SS	21	0	0	0	9	8	23	24	1	0.0	9.8	25	45.3%	.365
2021 FS	SEA	MLB	23	2	2	0	57	0	50	48	7	3.3	7.3	40	40.2%	.282

Comparables: Sam Gaviglio, Luis Perdomo, Humberto Mejía

Another iteration of the Jerry Dipoto Advanced Right-Handed College Draft Pick-O-Matic, the Kirby Model features the same upper 90's fastball as is now standard with the line. It also features a customized Carlos Silva-Walk Reduction Valve (patent pending), which has kept Kirby from issuing a walk as a professional (albeit in only 23 official innings). Kirby's secondary stuff is a bit same-y and will probably never be better than average. His ability to stick in a major league rotation is going to come down to his ability to command that blazing heater, and not just in a way that "challenges" rookie league hitters with pure velocity down the pipe. If he does, he's got center-of-rotation upside. If he doesn't, well, bullpens need pitchers too.

YEAR	TEAM	LVL	AGE	WHIP	ERA	DRA-	WARP	MPH	FB%	WHF	CSP
2019	EVE	SS	21	1.04	2.35	72	0.5				
2021 FS	SEA	MLB	23	1.35	4.40	104	0.1				

Wyatt Mills RHP
Born: 01/25/95 Age: 26 Bats: R Throws: R
Height: 6'4" Weight: 190 Origin: Round 3, 2017 Draft (#93 overall)

YEAR	TEAM	LVL	AGE	W	L	SV	G	GS	IP	H	HR	BB/9	K/9	K	GB%	BABIP
2018	MOD	HI-A	23	6	0	11	35	0	42^1	29	1	1.9	10.4	49	52.9%	.280
2018	ARK	AA	23	0	2	0	9	0	10^2	18	0	3.4	8.4	10	42.5%	.450
2019	ARK	AA	24	4	2	8	41	0	52^2	43	2	2.9	11.3	66	52.7%	.320
2021 FS	SEA	MLB	26	2	2	0	57	0	50	43	6	3.9	9.5	52	46.1%	.281
2021 DC	SEA	MLB	26	0	0	0	17	0	17.7	15	2	3.9	9.5	18	46.1%	.281

Comparables: Matt Foster, JD Hammer, Cody Ege

Some pitchers have changeups; some relievers, just by entering the game with a different look, basically *are* changeups. With a name like a secondary character from *Tombstone*, it's appropriate that Mills fires the ball from the hip. Look for him and his blazing sidearm to bring some justice to the AL West in 2021.

YEAR	TEAM	LVL	AGE	WHIP	ERA	DRA-	WARP	MPH	FB%	WHF	CSP
2018	MOD	HI-A	23	0.90	1.91	71	0.7				
2018	ARK	AA	23	2.06	10.12	80	0.1				
2019	ARK	AA	24	1.14	4.27	88	0.2				
2021 FS	SEA	MLB	26	1.30	4.00	95	0.4				
2021 DC	SEA	MLB	26	1.30	4.00	95	0.1				

Aríel Miranda LHP
Born: 01/10/89 Age: 32 Bats: L Throws: L
Height: 6'2" Weight: 190 Origin: International Free Agent, 2015

YEAR	TEAM	LVL	AGE	W	L	SV	G	GS	IP	H	HR	BB/9	K/9	K	GB%	BABIP
2018	TAC	AAA	29	5	0	0	10	9	45^1	44	3	4.8	7.9	40	34.8%	.318
2018	FKU	NPB	29	6	1	0	8	8	47^2	28	3	5.0	7.6	40		
2018	SEA	MLB	29	0	0	0	1	1	5	6	0	7.2	9.0	5	40.0%	.400
2019	FKU	NPB	30	7	5	0	18		86	80	13	5.0	6.1	58		
2020	CTB	CPBL	31	10	8	0	26	26	160^1	150	14	3.4	9.8	175		
2021									No projection							

Comparables: Nick Tropeano, Wily Peralta, Chad Bettis

A foreign southpaw like De Paula, Miranda was another new addition to the Brothers' rotation prior to the 2020 season. A veteran of the Cuban National Series before signing with the Orioles in 2015, Miranda's experience spans beyond the 200+ innings he threw for Baltimore and Seattle in the latter half of the 2010s, as well as parts of two seasons with the Fukuoka Softbank Hawks. With the Brothers last year he was able to step in and co-anchor the pitching staff with De Paula. Third in the league in ERA and second in strikeout rate among qualified starters, Miranda spun a gem in Game 3 of the Taiwan Series, throwing a three-hit complete game against the Lions. It was enough to earn him a promotion, as he'll spend 2021 with the Doosan Bears of the KBO.

YEAR	TEAM	LVL	AGE	WHIP	ERA	DRA-	WARP	MPH	FB%	WHF	CSP
2018	TAC	AAA	29	1.50	3.97	107	0.3				
2018	FKU	NPB	29	1.15	1.89						
2018	SEA	MLB	29	2.00	1.80	132	0.0	93.0	59.8%	27.5%	
2019	FKU	NPB	30	1.49	4.19						
2020	CTB	CPBL	31	1.32	3.70						
2021						No projection					

Seattle Mariners 2021

Andres Muñoz   RHP

Born: 01/16/99   Age: 22   Bats: R   Throws: R
Height: 6'2"   Weight: 243   Origin: International Free Agent, 2015

YEAR	TEAM	LVL	AGE	W	L	SV	G	GS	IP	H	HR	BB/9	K/9	K	GB%	BABIP
2018	TRI	SS	19	0	0	0	5	0	5^2	0	0	3.2	14.3	9	42.9%	.000
2018	SA	AA	19	2	1	7	20	0	19	11	0	5.2	9.0	19	54.5%	.250
2019	AMA	AA	20	0	2	4	16	0	16^2	9	1	5.9	18.4	34	40.7%	.320
2019	ELP	AAA	20	3	2	2	19	0	19	16	3	3.3	11.4	24	51.1%	.317
2019	SD	MLB	20	1	1	1	22	0	23	16	2	4.3	11.7	30	39.3%	.264
2021 FS	SEA	MLB	22	2	2	0	57	0	50	41	6	4.2	10.6	58	43.8%	.287
2021 DC	SEA	MLB	22	0	0	0	11	0	23.7	19	3	4.2	10.6	28	43.8%	.287

Comparables: Ryan Wagner, Miguel Castro, Luiz Gohara

Before he was sidelined with Tommy John surgery in spring, Muñoz had an 80-grade fastball and a future as a top-tier closer. The degree to which he recovers this heat correlates directly to the chances that history will refer not to the "Austin Nola trade" but to the "Andrés Muñoz trade."

YEAR	TEAM	LVL	AGE	WHIP	ERA	DRA-	WARP	MPH	FB%	WHF	CSP
2018	TRI	SS	19	0.35	0.00	187	-0.3				
2018	SA	AA	19	1.16	0.95	68	0.4				
2019	AMA	AA	20	1.20	2.16	42	0.5				
2019	ELP	AAA	20	1.21	3.79	59	0.6				
2019	SD	MLB	20	1.17	3.91	81	0.3	101.9	68.0%	31.8%	
2021 FS	SEA	MLB	22	1.31	3.89	88	0.6	101.9	68.0%	31.8%	45.9%
2021 DC	SEA	MLB	22	1.31	3.89	88	0.3	101.9	68.0%	31.8%	45.9%

Drew Steckenrider   RHP

Born: 01/10/91   Age: 30   Bats: R   Throws: R
Height: 6'4"   Weight: 217   Origin: Round 8, 2012 Draft (#257 overall)

YEAR	TEAM	LVL	AGE	W	L	SV	G	GS	IP	H	HR	BB/9	K/9	K	GB%	BABIP
2018	MIA	MLB	27	4	4	5	71	0	64^2	55	7	3.8	10.3	74	33.7%	.296
2019	MIA	MLB	28	0	2	0	15	0	14^1	9	6	3.1	8.8	14	31.6%	.094
2021 FS	SEA	MLB	30	2	2	0	57	0	50	41	7	3.6	10.0	55	36.9%	.274

Comparables: Dominic Leone, Shawn Armstrong, Hansel Robles

Just two years ago, Steckenrider looked like a dominant late-inning reliever, or perhaps even a future closer. He missed most of 2019 and all of 2020 with elbow problems, and was outrighted and declared free agency after the season.

YEAR	TEAM	LVL	AGE	WHIP	ERA	DRA-	WARP	MPH	FB%	WHF	CSP
2018	MIA	MLB	27	1.27	3.90	99	0.4	96.5	76.4%	25.3%	
2019	MIA	MLB	28	0.98	6.28	121	-0.1	96.2	62.0%	21.4%	
2021 FS	SEA	MLB	30	1.23	3.52	85	0.7	96.4	72.2%	24.1%	50.1%

Juan Then RHP

Born: 02/07/00   Age: 21   Bats: R   Throws: R
Height: 6'1"   Weight: 175   Origin: International Free Agent, 2016

YEAR	TEAM	LVL	AGE	W	L	SV	G	GS	IP	H	HR	BB/9	K/9	K	GB%	BABIP
2018	YAE	ROK	18	0	3	0	11	11	50	38	2	2.0	7.6	42	45.4%	.259
2019	MAR	ROK	19	0	0	0	1	0	2	2	0	0.0	9.0	2	20.0%	.400
2019	EVE	SS	19	0	3	0	7	6	30[1]	24	1	2.7	9.5	32	34.6%	.299
2019	WV	LO-A	19	1	2	0	3	3	16	7	1	2.2	7.9	14	29.3%	.150
2021 FS	SEA	MLB	21	2	2	0	57	0	50	47	7	3.6	7.7	42	38.0%	.282

Comparables: Rony García, Luis Severino, Antonio Santos

One of the many members of the "Dipoto Takesy Backsies Program," Then was shipped off to New York, only to be re-acquired by Seattle. Unlike most of the players in this fraternity, the slightly-built right-hander may have been well worth the effort, or at least he just made good use of his time during the exchange program. Stll only 21, Then will look to push his power arsenal to the mid-minors in 2021. Should he build off the success he showed in 2019, his place in Seattle's Top 10 prospects list (no small feat these days) will be secure.

YEAR	TEAM	LVL	AGE	WHIP	ERA	DRA-	WARP	MPH	FB%	WHF	CSP
2018	YAE	ROK	18	0.98	2.70						
2019	MAR	ROK	19	1.00	0.00						
2019	EVE	SS	19	1.09	3.56	65	0.7				
2019	WV	LO-A	19	0.69	2.25	59	0.4				
2021 FS	SEA	MLB	21	1.34	4.26	99	0.3				

Will Vest   RHP

Born: 06/06/95   Age: 26   Bats: R   Throws: R
Height: 6'0"   Weight: 180   Origin: Round 12, 2017 Draft (#365 overall)

YEAR	TEAM	LVL	AGE	W	L	SV	G	GS	IP	H	HR	BB/9	K/9	K	GB%	BABIP
2018	WM	LO-A	23	3	4	5	20	0	35^1	43	0	3.1	11.2	44	53.9%	.422
2018	LAK	HI-A	23	1	0	0	10	0	13^1	16	1	1.4	8.1	12	53.3%	.349
2019	LAK	HI-A	24	1	1	3	14	0	21^1	9	1	3.0	12.7	30	46.3%	.205
2019	ERI	AA	24	2	4	4	20	0	27	31	4	3.0	8.3	25	43.4%	.342
2019	TOL	AAA	24	0	0	1	3	0	6^2	9	1	2.7	4.0	3	63.6%	.381
2021 FS	SEA	MLB	26	2	2	0	57	0	50	46	7	4.0	8.4	46	43.7%	.282
2021 DC	SEA	MLB	26	1	2	0	40	0	41.7	39	6	4.0	8.4	38	43.7%	.282

Comparables: Steve Hathaway, Tyler Rogers, Chad Girodo

Vest (who does not go by William but will be treated as such by this comment for the pure sake of pun avoidance) allegedly built up his fastball velocity in 2020 to form a combination with an already-decent breaking ball, providing the upside of a seventh-inning guy. The problem with using a Rule 5 pick on a middle reliever is that one of their principle virtues is their fungibility; teams have to rotate fresh arms to Triple-A and back. Vest can probably justify his lack of flexibility, however, given the rest of the Mariners' bullpen.

YEAR	TEAM	LVL	AGE	WHIP	ERA	DRA-	WARP	MPH	FB%	WHF	CSP
2018	WM	LO-A	23	1.56	4.84	72	0.6				
2018	LAK	HI-A	23	1.35	6.08	94	0.1				
2019	LAK	HI-A	24	0.75	0.84	56	0.5				
2019	ERI	AA	24	1.48	5.33	121	-0.4				
2019	TOL	AAA	24	1.65	2.70	155	-0.1				
2021 FS	SEA	MLB	26	1.38	4.50	104	0.1				
2021 DC	SEA	MLB	26	1.38	4.50	104	0.1				

Mariners Prospects

The State of the System:
The system is too good now to indulge in our usual trope of a sad Death Cab for Cutie lyric here. Maybe there's a happy Death Cab song, we don't know. Frankly, we don't want to know.

The Top Ten:

─────── ★ ★ ★ *2021 Top 101 Prospect* **#3** ★ ★ ★ ───────

1 **Julio Y. Rodríguez OF**   OFP: 70   ETA: Late 2021/Early 2022
Born: 12/29/00   Age: 20   Bats: R   Throws: R   Height: 6'3"   Weight: 180
Origin: International Free Agent, 2017

The Report: Here's the one sentence version of this report: Rodríguez hits the ball harder than any other prospect in any system.

The longer version adds some more feats of strength. Rodríguez played the entire 2019 season at age 18. He was one of the best hitters in the Low-A South Atlantic League for the bulk of the season, then went up and torched High-A for a few weeks at the end, then shined in the Arizona Fall League. His swing is compact and quick, and he's starting to lift the ball more in a way that belies future high-end power. He manages the strike zone very well, with an extremely advanced approach for his age. He's an above-average runner, and though we think his defensive profile will play best in right given his excellent arm, he has some chance to play center too.

Development Track: The only downside we can find is that he's missed a good deal of time with injuries. Rodríguez was out for a couple months in 2019 with a hand injury from a hit-by-pitch, and he missed some time this summer from a wrist injury from baserunning practice. What we heard and saw of his 2020 developmental time was loud enough that we're still bumping him up.

Variance: Medium. The injuries and lack of pro experience are, I guess, slight concerns. But you can make a cogent argument that Rodríguez is the best prospect in baseball right now.

Mark Barry's Fantasy Take: Do you like really good baseball players that are really good at hitting baseballs? I don't know that he'll run for very much longer (or with a ton of volume), but it wouldn't shock me to see future seasons of .300/35 homers, perhaps even near futures. Do whatever you can to get Julio Rodríguez on your fantasy team.

─────── ★ ★ ★ *2021 Top 101 Prospect* **#6** ★ ★ ★ ───────

2. Jarred Kelenic   OF   OFP: 70   ETA: 2021
Born: 07/16/99   Age: 21   Bats: L   Throws: L   Height: 6'1"   Weight: 190
Origin: Round 1, 2018 Draft (#6 overall)

The Report: Kelenic has a classic lefty swing. He's got a very good chance to be at least a plus hit, plus power player based on his improved bat path and move to the ball. He has an advanced plate approach, and because of that and how quickly he advanced in 2019, we're confident he'll hit in the majors, about as much as we can be for a prospect who hasn't played in the majors yet and has fewer than 100 plate appearances in the upper minors.

Kelenic is a plus runner at present, and combined with his plus arm he has a shot to remain in center field long term. He's going to have to improve routes and closing instincts to stick there long-term, and with all the competition in the Seattle outfield picture it's quite possible he ends up in a corner anyway. He'd project extremely well in either right or left.

Development Track: We are not at all down on Kelenic even though he's no longer the top prospect in the system. He's moving up, not down, on the Top 101 list. Seattle had one of the more open alternate site and instructs setups, posting quite a bit of video and TrackMan data on their team social media accounts, and nothing we saw has us down on Kelenic at all. He's still on track to be a great player and be up next year. We just have an even better (if only slightly so) projection on Rodríguez right now.

Variance: Medium. Low on that bat in and of itself, higher on the chance that he has to slide to a corner, where hitting a 70 OFP is a really high offensive bar.

Mark Barry's Fantasy Take: Though I also like Rodríguez slightly more, I wouldn't really put up too much of a fight if you prefer Kelenic for your fantasy roster. Kelenic is a great hitter, he's polished, and he might even steal 15 bases for you, at least in the short term. Both of these two are top-five options in dynasty, which is pretty exciting if you're a Mariners fan.

─────── ★ ★ ★ *2021 Top 101 Prospect* **#38** ★ ★ ★ ───────

3. Logan Gilbert   RHP   OFP: 60   ETA: 2021
Born: 05/05/97   Age: 24   Bats: R   Throws: R   Height: 6'6"   Weight: 225
Origin: Round 1, 2018 Draft (#14 overall)

The Report: Gilbert is a polished, four-pitch college righty who got a little more velocity in his first full pro season and saw his profile bump into the top half of the 101. There's no 70-grade bullet in the arsenal, but he commands four above-average or better pitches, with the curve having plus swing-and-miss projection. His arsenal plays up given the advanced pitchability and despite his height, Gilbert repeats everything well and gets good extension. Is he the most exciting pitching prospect in baseball? No. Is he likely to be a good mid-rotation starter as soon as 2021? Yep.

Development Track: I suspect in a more normal season, Gilbert could have very well pitched himself into a late season call-up, given the Double-A success he already had in 2019. Instead, he pitched at the alternate site and waits to see how the Mariners rotation mix shakes out in 2021. If he's not ready on Opening Day, I'd expect him up as soon as there is a spot.

Variance: Low. Look, there's a reason I shy away from calling any pitching prospect "safe" or even "high-floor." But Gilbert checks every box to be an above-average major league starter in the near term.

Mark Barry's Fantasy Take: Under normal circumstances, we probably would have seen Gilbert on the bump at Safeco at some point in 2020. I might be a touch lower on Gilbert than most, but there's no-doubt he's one of the 10-best pitching prospects in baseball, I'm just not sold on the ceiling.

--- ★ ★ ★ *2021 Top 101 Prospect* **#50** ★ ★ ★ ---

4
Emerson Hancock   RHP   OFP: 60   ETA: 2022
Born: 05/31/99   Age: 22   Bats: R   Throws: R   Height: 6'4"   Weight: 213
Origin: Round 1, 2020 Draft (#6 overall)

The Report: It's hard to build a more ideal pitching prospect at the top of the draft. Hancock, who one scout said would have been a top-10 pick if he were draft eligible after his sophomore year, fulfilled that destiny a year later, becoming the third straight college pitcher chosen in the first round by Seattle. While the previous two are known for their plus command/control and good stuff, Hancock not only satisfies the plus command, but the stuff is arguably the best of the bunch. Featuring a fastball that sits comfortably mid-90s and can touch higher, he also brings a slider and changeup that flash plus and a curveball that isn't far behind. His ability to control his body through the delivery and play off each of his pitches with advanced control is seldom found in college. Last but not least, he has the ready-made build of a future front-line starter. Literally every box is checked.

Development Track: Sure, there is plenty to ogle at on Hancock's scouting sheet, but it hasn't always been smooth sailing during his collegiate days. He took his lumps his freshman year, dealt with a minor injury the following season, and didn't get off to a fast beginning of his abbreviated draft year. All signs point toward what you want to see out of a top draft pick, yet there still is that prickly pickiness of wanting to see more. Assuming we see around 20-plus starts and over 100 innings in 2021, he will quickly shoot up preference lists.

Variance: Medium. Barring something catastrophic happening (go ahead and find some wood to knock on as you read this), Hancock has everything needed to remain a starter. Maybe the stuff backs up, but even then he's probably a number four in a rotation.

Mark Barry's Fantasy Take: I'm typically more likely to roll the dice on a guy like Hancock than Gilbert. Hancock isn't as polished, and he's not as close, but I think there's more strikeout upside, and with it, a better likelihood that he can be a front-of-the-rotation ace.

──────── ★ ★ ★ *2021 Top 101 Prospect* **#72** ★ ★ ★ ────────

5 **Taylor Trammell   CF**   OFP: 60   ETA: 2021
Born: 09/13/97   Age: 23   Bats: L   Throws: L   Height: 6'2"   Weight: 213
Origin: Round 1, 2016 Draft (#35 overall)

The Report: Trammell has long been a divisive prospect. At his best, he projects as a center fielder with plus hit and power tools. At other times he looks like a bench outfielder who might be limited to left. The culprit here is a swing that has undergone several tweaks and even overhauls, both in Cincy and then in San Diego. Trammell didn't hit for average or power in Double-A in 2019 and played mostly left field, as his arm is well-below average. He's a plus-plus runner though and the outfield instincts are good enough to stick in center otherwise.

Development Track: It's unusual for a top prospect to get traded twice before debuting in the majors. It's more unusual for that second trade to be for a 30-year-old catcher who had fewer than 400 plate appearances. You can look at this a couple ways. Two teams have looked to offload Trammell. But two teams have also tried to acquire him. The Mariners have already started fiddling with his swing some more, and he did flash that plus raw power again at the alternate site and instructs, but his inconsistency at the plate continues.

Variance: High. It's unclear exactly when the tradition of the Captain going down with the ship began. It's often traced back to the sinking of the HMS Birkenhead, immortalized in the Rudyard Kipling poem "Soldier an' Sailor Too."

Mark Barry's Fantasy Take: It's a little worrying that Trammell is already on his third team at the ripe old age of 23, but since I'm the sunniest of sunny optimists, I'll take that to mean there are just multiple teams that value his skill set. The fantasy upside for Trammell is still there as a high-OBP guy that can steal bases and at least contribute in four categories. The likelihood of him reaching that upside might have diminished slightly, however.

★ ★ ★ *2021 Top 101 Prospect* **#68** ★ ★ ★

6

George Kirby   RHP   OFP: 60   ETA: 2022
Born: 02/04/98   Age: 23   Bats: R   Throws: R   Height: 6'4"   Weight: 215
Origin: Round 1, 2019 Draft (#20 overall)

The Report: With a broadly similar profile to Gilbert coming out of the draft, Kirby featured plus-plus command of an otherwise average-to-solid-average four pitch mix. An elite strikethrower in a calendar year across the Cape, his draft season at Elon, and his first pro summer in the Northwest League, he posted a 156:7 K:BB ratio in 124 ⅓ innings. It would be fair to ask what the ultimate upside was at this point. Command is not an out pitch, and while Kirby's arsenal was fine, there wasn't an obvious plus pitch projection. Then Kirby showed up this spring sitting more mid-90s than low-90s without losing any of the command. OK, now we're cooking with some gas.

Development Track: Kirby technically hasn't seen full-season ball yet, but I don't see a particularly good reason to start him lower than Advanced-A in 2021, and I wouldn't be shocked if he kicks off in the Texas League. He could be a major league factor as soon as this season, but a full year getting him accustomed to a pro workload and schedule isn't the worst idea in the world.

Variance: Medium. Kirby has a lot of the same positive markers as a starter as Gilbert. He even has a few more ticks on the fastball now. He also has far less pro experience.

Mark Barry's Fantasy Take: Gilbert and Hancock are definitely the marquee arms in this org, but Kirby might be my personal favorite. Admittedly, I'm a sucker for high control/command guys, and Kirby definitely fits that bill. It also seems like there's a chance his 2020 development could have raised his ceiling, and his dynasty cost will certainly be lower than the team's other big arms.

7

Noelvi Marte   SS   OFP: 60   ETA: 2024
Born: 10/16/01   Age: 19   Bats: R   Throws: R   Height: 6'1"   Weight: 181
Origin: International Free Agent, 2018

The Report / Development Track: One of the pain points for our 2021 lists is if I already wrote a navel-gazing, process-oriented blurb about a recent big bonus IFA with no stateside experience in 2020, I don't really have anything to fall back on this time around. And we do have slightly more information about Marte, who was both at the Mariners' alternate site and instructs. He ended up literally being the last cut off our 101—we have an orphan blurb and everything—because we think the bat will play to at least above-average on both hit and power, and he's likely to stick at shortstop. That's the type of profile that makes our national list. But while we have more information about Marte, it's hard to say we have enough information about Marte.

Variance: Extreme. Our old generic risk profile would look something like this—complex-league resume, uncertainty about the long term hit tool projection, needs to prove it against better competition.

Mark Barry's Fantasy Take: Your mileage may vary on Marte, or guys like Marte. Part of the dynasty-league fun is identifying "The Next Guy", and after a breakout 2019, Marte shot up a ton of fantasy lists for just that reason. The only problem is that his experience stateside has been limited to Mariners camp in non-competitive situations. That's fine, but there's still a lot we don't know, and with guys like Marte, you can't wait around to find out. Marte could be very, very good, but I'd be more likely to take advantage of his shiny "Next" status and cash in for someone that could help sooner.

8 Juan Then RHP   OFP: 60   ETA: 2023
Born: 02/07/00   Age: 21   Bats: R   Throws: R   Height: 6'1"   Weight: 175
Origin: International Free Agent, 2016

The Report: Then is on his second spell as a Mariners prospect—the Dipoto special—but the version that came back from the Yankees was better than the one traded away. The undersized righty comfortably sits mid-90s with a potential above-average curve and change as well. It's not the easiest velocity given his size, but the mechanics aren't prohibitive for a starter.

Development Track: We predicted a bump in velocity in this space last year and Then is running his fastball into the upper-90s more now. We don't know how the velocity holds up over a full season, and he's on the shorter and slighter side. There's the makings of a deep enough arsenal to start, but there will always be the temptation to fast track him as a power relief arm. Then will only be 21, so keeping him stretched out for the starter's reps in the near term makes the most sense. And hey, sometimes the starter stays a starter longer than you'd think.

Variance: Very High. Then's career high in innings pitched is 61, which came in 2017 in the Dominican Summer League. He has yet to pitch above A-ball and the frame is ... uh, not a traditional starter's build.

Mark Barry's Fantasy Take: Last year, I took a "wait and see" approach with Then, and then, well, 2020 happened. I still don't know if Then needs to be on your dynasty radar quite yet, but if you wanted to toss him on a watch list, I wouldn't argue.

9 Cal Raleigh C   OFP: 55   ETA: Late 2021 / 2022
Born: 11/26/96   Age: 24   Bats: S   Throws: R   Height: 6'3"   Weight: 215
Origin: Round 3, 2018 Draft (#90 overall)

The Report: Raleigh was drafted as a bat-first, switch-hitting catcher with potential plus pop, but quickly made strides behind the plate as well to get his defense past passable and in the average range. The power plays from both sides, and while there's swing-and-miss concerns that might limit the batting averages to .240 or .250, the bat speed and loft should get Raleigh 20 or so bombs a year. He's unspectacular defensively but he moves and receives well, although the throwing arm is a bit light.

Development Track: Raleigh went to the alternate site for 2020, and currently sits third on the catching depth chart for Seattle behind the likely MLB tandem of Tom Murphy and Luis Torrens. Murphy provides a good model for what a good major league outcome might look like for Raleigh, a bigger framed catcher with raw power, who gets just enough of it into games, and who worked himself into a good enough defender to be a solid 1A or 1B catcher. That might have to wait a season though as you'd like to see a consolidation period against upper minors pitching first.

Variance: Medium. The stiffness in the swing might get exposed against better pitching—and that K-rate in the first pass of Double-A was a little worrisome—limiting Raleigh to more of a backup with a bit of pop. But the bar for catcher offense is low enough that even an OBP that flirts with the wrong side of .300 doesn't mean he's not a viable regular if the pop and glove plays.

Mark Barry's Fantasy Take: I could see tossing a buck on Raleigh at the end of an auction in a two-catcher draft. Whether that buck is well spent, however, is questionable.

10 Zach DeLoach

OFP: 50   ETA: 2023
Born: 08/18/98   Age: 22   Bats: L   Throws: R   Height: 6'1"   Weight: 205
Origin: Round 2, 2020 Draft (#43 overall)

The Report: What exactly are the Mariners getting with their second round pick out of Texas A&M? Are they getting the mediocre offensive player with good physical tools from his first two years in the SEC? Or the juggernaut who lit up summer wood-bat leagues and torched subpar pitching during his brief spring? DeLoach is two sides of the same coin and it's tough to tell which direction the production levels will go next. The fact he has a proven record excelling with wood bats is helpful, showing excellent power potential to the pull side. He's also been a good runner at times, although some added bulk may start weighing that down, and he's already been playing more corner outfield than center.

Development Track: DeLoach is going to have to prove the newfound hitting ability is real. Every draft pick has some element of, "prove it, rook" to back up why they were taken. He will need to do that and then some. Assuming the changes to the swing—he's more closed off than he was before, which seems to help quiet his movements and track the ball better—remain from when he was at his best, it won't seem like such a buy-high pick after all.

Variance: Medium. He's unlikely to rock the boat too much one way or the other. He's not as bad as he was early in his college days, and he's not playing on God Mode, either. Something in-between that seems far more realistic.

Mark Barry's Fantasy Take: It doesn't take much for good-not-great upside to slide into the realm of fourth outfielders.

The Prospects You Meet Outside The Top Ten

Interesting 2019 draft follows

Brandon Williamson LHP Born: 04/02/98 Age: 23 Bats: L Throws: L Height: 6'6" Weight: 210 Origin: Round 2, 2019 Draft (#59 overall)
Williamson certainly has a case to slot onto the back of the top ten somewhere. A four-pitch lefty whose 6-foot-6 frame creates a touch angle on his low-90s fastball, he also has two viable breaking ball looks already. The change needs some work, and Williamson has a very limited pro track record, but there's the makings of a backend starter with some projection past that.

Isaiah Campbell RHP Born: 08/15/97 Age: 23 Bats: R Throws: R Height: 6'4" Weight: 225 Origin: Round 2, 2019 Draft (#76 overall)
Campbell could also claim that he was passed over for a top ten spot. There's more reliever risk here, as he already has the 95 mph, the slider, and a college elbow injury on his resume. After a heavy workload his draft year at Arkansas, the Mariners elected not to have him pitch in 2019, so he still hasn't officially made his pro debut—although he did pitch at the alternate site. There's just a bit more mystery here than players like DeLoach or Raleigh.

Interesting 2020 draft follows

Connor Phillips Born: 05/04/01 Age: 20 Bats: R Throws: R Height: 6'2" Weight: 190 Origin: Round CBB, 2020 Draft (#64 overall)
Phillips decided to forgo his LSU commitment to go to junior college, and ended up getting picked by Seattle in the Comp B round. He has a very live arm, showing at times upper-90s velocity, but the radar gun readings can be inconsistent. The delivery is very upper-body heavy—which may explain the wide fastball range—and he's a bit of a project. I suppose you can't spell projectable without "project" though, and Phillips is projectable too. Still, I get reliever vibes here.

MLB-ready relievers

Sam Delaplane RHP Born: 03/27/95 Age: 26 Bats: R Throws: R Height: 5'11" Weight: 175 Origin: Round 23, 2017 Draft (#693 overall)
I'm a little disappointed we didn't get to see Delaplane in the majors if only to see how ludicrous the pitch data was. The fastball/breaking ball combo on paper is plus/plus, but there's late life/bite that has led to some video game-like strikeout numbers in the minors. We'll have to wait until 2021 to see him unleashed in the majors, but he's likely a ready-made seventh/eighth inning type.

MLB arms, but less upside than you'd like

Ljay Newsome RHP Born: 11/08/96 Age: 24 Bats: R Throws: R Height: 5'11" Weight: 210 Origin: Round 26, 2015 Draft (#785 overall)
A personal cheeseball made good. Newsome was an extreme control artist in the minors who bumped his fastball from the upper-80s to the low-90s, which paired with an average enough breaking ball and change, racked up strikeouts in the minors in 2019. That last step is the steepest though, and his major league fate—albeit in a very small sample—was not uncommon for prospect arms whose control far outpaces their stuff. When in the zone, Newsome got hit hard, which led to a bit more nibbling, a few more walks, and far less whiffs. He might be crowded out of the Mariners' rotation plans, if he was ever really in them to begin with, but he might still be a useful utility arm. I'll be rooting for him anyway.

Prospects to dream on a little

Austin Shenton 3B Born: 01/22/98 Age: 23 Bats: L Throws: R Height: 6'0" Weight: 195 Origin: Round 5, 2019 Draft (#156 overall)
The rare projectable college bat, Shenton can really hit. There were two main questions with the profile. Would he be able to tap into his raw power given the shortness of the swing. Well he did hit a bomb over the ridiculous center field fence in Tacoma last summer. The other question is his ultimate defensive home, which remains undetermined. He was our low minors sleeper last year. So let's run that back.

Alberto Rodriguez RF Born: 10/06/00 Age: 20 Bats: L Throws: L Height: 5'11" Weight: 180 Origin: International Free Agent, 2017
The player to be named later in the Taijuan Walker deal, Rodriguez can also really hit. His ultimate defensive home is probably left field though, as his arm is below-average and he doesn't have the foot speed for center. He hits the ball incredibly hard, but that might not translate into plus game power. Still, he can really hit, so keep an eye on him.

Top Talents 25 and Under (as of 4/1/2021):

1. Julio Rodríguez, OF
2. Jarred Kelenic, OF
3. Kyle Lewis, OF
4. Logan Gilbert, RHP
5. Emerson Hancock, RHP
6. Justus Sheffield, LHP
7. Taylor Trammell, OF

8. George Kirby, RHP
9. Noelvi Marte, SS
10. Evan White, 1B

Kyle Lewis deservedly won the AL Rookie of the Year award, marking off another step on a phenomenal ascension. He cut his strikeout rate and raised his walk rate, and his performance was driven by all-around offense instead of an all-or-nothing power spike. This level of production is probably sustainable for him moving forward, and though it's not totally clear how the outfield spots in Seattle will shake out positionally quite yet, Lewis has made himself a major part of the mix.

Just a year after being demoted to Double-A, Justus Sheffield took a regular turn in the Seattle rotation. He's remade himself as something of a sinkerballer, and he doesn't quite throw as hard as he did as a prospect, but the plus slider is still there and the changeup has shown some late development. He's probably settling in as a mid-rotation starter, although given his previous bouts of wildness and ineffectiveness we'd like to see everything hold together for longer than a couple months.

Evan White and Justin Dunn occupy a similar space as players who had horrid 2020s. White, who looked for all the world like he was ready to be a quality major-league hitter, instead hit .176 in the first year of his long-term contract. Dunn also took a regular rotation turn, but walked more than six batters per 9 and posted a 7.46 DRA. White was a better prospect and Dunn might be headed for relief, so I ranked White here; Dunn would've been about 12th or 13th.

Part 3: Featured Articles

Mariners All-Time Top 10 Players

by Patrick Dubuque

POSITION PLAYERS

ALVIN DAVIS, 1B (1984-1991)
For those who arrived at their Mariners fandom later, it can be difficult to explain why it was Davis that earned the nickname of "Mr. Mariner." He made one All-Star game, after all, posted a career isolated slugging percentage equal to Dave Henderson's, and was finished by the age of 29. Bill James used Davis as his example for what he called "old player skills," hypothesizing that hitters who relied on walks and power, rather than speed and athleticism, were likely to collapse early. Such a collapse infers a distance to fall, however, and for eight years he was a consistent producer and leader for a club that often lacked both. For a franchise that spent its first decade trading any player who might ask for a raise, the former 1984 Rookie of the Year provided an actual presence, a magnetism that pulled in hope. If The Kid saved baseball in Seattle, Davis made the idea even possible, anchoring the lineup and providing something that could actually be built around.

BRET BOONE, 2B (1992-1993, 2001-2005)
Ichiro may have been the soul of the record-setting 2001 Mariners, but no one was more emblematic of the team's startling accomplishment than Boone. An M's prospect traded early in his career for one of the city's most beloved (Dan Wilson) and despised (Bobby Ayala) players, Boone spent his twenties wandering the league as a second-division starter, providing pop for a second baseman but also low batting averages and inconsistent defense. Welcomed back as a stopgap, the Mariners instead received one of the best three-year stretches in team history. Years before regression to the mean became a cliché, Boone hit

.343/.373/.479 in April of 2001 and got yet hotter after that, finishing third in MVP voting. Neither player nor team got to enjoy their greatness for long, but what a moment it was.

ROBINSON CANÓ, 2B (2014-2018)

It should have been a disaster: A second baseman in his thirties signing a ten-year, quarter-$1 billion contract, banishing himself to baseball's geographic and productive backwater. He failed to end the team's deepening playoff drought and spent half a year suspended for steroid use during the team's single best shot to end it. And yet for all that, Canó's time in Seattle, much like the free-agent-oriented strategy of general manager Jack Zduriencik, was a relative, if insufficient, success. Despite the aging curves of second baseman before him, Canó performed ably with both the stick and the glove and earned the devotion of Mariners fans forever by being traded for top prospect Jared Kelenic. The future tense of that past moment is so strong that people even now might consider the signing a mistake, but it was the kind of overpay that most fans wish their teams would even consider now.

KYLE SEAGER, 3B (2011-PRESENT)

The pandemic-shortened season of 2020 denied Seager the opportunity to post his ninth consecutive 20-homer season, though it should be noted that in his 60 games, he was on pace. That 60 is an equally important number: A 2019 season marred by a spring hand injury was the only one in his career that he failed to start 90 percent of his team's games since 2011. In a decade of Mariners baseball synonymous with failure, shifting organizational philosophy, and more failure, Seager remains as the club's lone fixture and quiet clubhouse leader. He arrived in the shadow of college teammate Dustin Ackley and always camouflaged himself behind whatever new free agent, rookie, or motto the team has marketed forth. And yet he's not only the greatest Seattle hitter of his decade, but likely one of the best to ever wear the uniform.

ADRIAN BELTRE, 3B (2005-2009)

Beltre's tour of duty came at the wrong time both for the Mariners and particularly for Mariners fans. Signed along with Richie Sexson in response to the swift and brutal demise of the team's unprecedented run of winning seasons and coming off a 48-home run season in Los Angeles, many found the future Hall of Famer a disappointment. After serving his contract, he would go on to Boston and enjoy a second-half surge that carried him to 3,166 hits and the inner circle of Cooperstown. But the timing was also unfortunate in that sabermetric literacy (and literature) of that time wasn't there to help fans appreciate how great those "disappointing" five years were, the true value of his Gold Glove defense and consistent ability to make contact. By the time Beltre's contract expired, Sexson was out of baseball and the team hadn't yet pulled itself out of its tailspin. With quarterbacks and point guards, great players make their teams great; for most baseball fans, great teams make their players great. No wonder that for Beltre, like so many others, "they always get better after they leave."

ALEX RODRIGUEZ, SS (1994-2000)

April 16, 2001 marked the first return of $252 million man Alex Rodriguez, wearing the red and blue of the Texas Rangers. Mariners fans were ready. They booed him lustily when he took the field in warmups, booed every plate appearance, even booed him in staccato when he caught the ball as it was going around the horn. Randy and Griffey had already gone out the door; the Mariners have always had to let their great ones go, with one notable exception. A-Rod was the youngest and best of them all, and anti-player sentiment was near its peak in the aftermath of steroids. He never really considered coming back. It was unforgivable. Rodriguez's five full seasons in Seattle have become a source of shared amnesia; Rodriguez eventually became a Yankee and a champion, and Mariners fans never found much reason to let their wounds go. Yet, during that half-decade A-Rod put in a pair of the greatest seasons that the franchise would or will ever see, including the second-ever 40/40. For all his future misdemeanors against steroids and broadcasting, he belongs next to the other faithless departed in the Mariners Ring of Honor. Demanding one's greats to stay 10 years in Seattle and swear fealty, as this list proves, makes for a pretty small ring.

JAY BUHNER, OF (1988-2001)

Buhner's outsized place in Seattle Mariners mythos stems primarily from moments off the field—the Seinfeld references, the buzz cut nights, the nickname, the continued radio presence—to the point where his actual production has almost become underrated. Arriving at the same time as Griffey, the pair locked down two-thirds of the outfield for a decade, offering stability for the lineup and for fans. He was the definition of a unidimensional player: His defense was generally atrocious, his speed was non-existent, and he was never even particularly good at staying healthy. And yet that one dimension made up for it, as home runs often do, and unlike Alvin Davis his old-player skills aged like sauerkraut, if not fine wine. For all the greats in Mariners history, only Buhner and Edgar stretch over the entire seven-year span of Mariners playoff history, and The Bone earned his place among those memories.

KEN GRIFFEY JR, OF (1989-1999, 2009-2010)

Even setting aside the numbers, no baseball player of the past 40 years was a bigger star than The Kid. Not Bonds, not Trout. Great athletes define their era, but figures like Griffey bend other eras toward their own; he made the 1980s feel stodgy and dated and supplied the model for energy and joy for the generations that came after. It's ironic that in his finest season, he played third wheel for the home run chase between McGwire and Sosa that revived the sport after the

1994 strike. After all, it was Griffey's talent and charisma that had made that resurrection possible, through the way he ushered in a generation of national fans. He also hit 398 home runs in a single decade, packing an entire Hall of Fame career into his twenties before dissipating into human form in far-off National League cities. If Ichiro is the model for the moment before the swing, Griffey's fluid, dynamic, lightsaber-swing follow through is pure kinetic energy. He could hit a ball in a way that pulled the cheers out of the crowd like the thunder of a nearby lightning strike. Some fans are quick to point out that for all the adulation, Griffey's end result was more "average Hall of Famer," and perhaps mathematically that's true. But there's a difference between being great and being a star, and The Kid was, unquestionably, both.

ICHIRO SUZUKI, OF (2001-2012, 2018-2019)

The way that Ichiro held his bat aloft, his left hand pinching at his jersey, tore him out of time itself. There are few distinctive stances in this overcoached age, but some, like Ichiro's, like Julio Franco's twisted coil or Sadaharu Oh's raised leg, encapsulate potential energy, a future moment about to happen and that will never really happen, over too soon, and the ball is in the air as we try to catch up. Ichiro's numbers place him among the greats, but aesthetically he has no living comparison. No one made it look easier than he did, the tiniest flick of the wrists and a ball landing softly, gently, thirty feet into the outfield. Ichiro is ageless; even as a coach, it seemed like he could sub himself in at any moment. But it's mostly that stance, forever perfect, forever ready, that pulls us back to its time, ready, excited for that next pitch.

EDGAR MARTINEZ, DH/3B (1987-2004)

There's a running joke about Edgar Martinez and baseball cards: They kept putting the wrong guy on them. His 1988 Donruss rookie card featured a mustachioed Edgar Diaz; his 1990 CMC card a clean shaven fellow Martinez, Tino. The Mariners seemed to struggle to put his face to a name as well, forcing him to sit in Triple-A while Jim Presley struck out again and again. It was only in his age-27 season (Griffey had hit 238 home runs by that age) that Edgar was given a full-time job, an organizational blind spot that nearly cost Martinez the counting stats needed for the Hall of Fame. It worked out in the end for all concerned, as Edgar doubled his way into Cooperstown and the Mariners into a franchise-saving 1995 ALDS Game 5 victory. Edgar's tenure with Seattle exuded professionalism, consistency, and pure hitting talent. He was one of the first to take the designated hitter position and change it from a last respite for the aged and defensively incapable to an offensive specialist.

PITCHERS

FLOYD BANNISTER, LHP (1979-1982)

It's hard to describe how cheap the early Mariners were; they're embarrassing even by the standards of modern tanking. They hated free agency, only attempting it to sign discounted, aging stars like Willie Horton and Jeff Burroughs with an eye more toward attendance than run production. These budgetary self-constraints, along with a fairly flimsy player development system, meant that the only means for generating excitement about a new season was to shuffle the hell out of some deck chairs, trading four or five players at a time. Most of these trades were lateral at best, but they nailed one, dealing away All-Star shortstop Craig Reynolds for a live-armed, inconsistent starter in Bannister. Though it didn't show in the win-loss totals at the time, the former first-overall pick was Seattle's first true ace. In 1982, when the team made a surprising run at .500, he led the AL in strikeouts, made the All-Star team… and hit free agency. He went and found (and easily earned) a five-year contract with the White Sox, and the Mariners went and found another chair.

JIM BEATTIE, RHP (1980-1986)

Never an ace even on the ace-less Mariners teams of the early 1980s, Beattie's career has been forgotten even by those few who witnessed it. Still, he serves as one sad archetype: The first of the many "what if" pitching careers to play in Seattle, ancestor of Brian Holman, Scott Bankhead, Gil Meche, and Brandon Morrow. After a slow start, Beattie seemed to improve every year, culminating in a 1984 season in which he completed 12 games (going 6-6 in them, because he was still a Mariner). Then tendonitis surfaced in his shoulder, he missed some time, and when he returned, he tore his rotator cuff and walked away. And yet, the story isn't wholly one of loss but also of redemption: Reaching the majors with the Yankees in 1978, he was publicly slagged by the owner for the crime of youthful inconsistency. "That kid pitching looked scared stiff," George Steinbrenner told the press after a shaky start against the Red Sox by the then 23-year-old. He had ordered that the kid be sent back to the minor leagues, not after the game, but now, mid-game. That Beattie got free and pitched well for the Mariners, even as briefly as he did, was the best revenge against a bully who did everything he could do destroy his own resources. After retirement, the Dartmouth product went back to school, got an MBA, and spent 25 years in various front offices where, it is hoped, he treated the kids under his authority better than he had been when he was their age.

MIKE MOORE, RHP (1982-1988)

Of the pre-Griffey era of the Seattle Mariners, no pitcher was more reviled than Moore. The 1981 first-overall draft-pick was given a scant 13 starts at Double-A during his draft year before being thrown to the wolves in the majors where fans and reporters carped on him for his inconsistency. Yet he was a solid starter in his second season and a quality number-two starter for years, a fact that was utterly ignored in favor of the win-loss records over which he had little control. In retrospect, Moore's relatively anonymous 14-year career is an achievement even for no. 1 picks. The greater problem is that because the Mariners have never dug much deeper than 1991 for team history, casually ignoring the 13 losing seasons that came before, Moore never received the reassessment in Seattle that he deserved. But then, Moore was happy to concentrate on later years as well. After leaving the Northwest, he signed on to the star-studded 1989 Oakland Athletics and quietly won a championship.

MARK LANGSTON, LHP (1984-1990)
The defining moment for Mark Langston in Mariners history is in opposition: Lying on his back, his glove held to his chest, after Luis Sojo slid under his tag to put away the 1995 play-in game that gave the team its first playoff appearance. It was also the defining moment for the Mariners in Mark Langston's history, given that the franchise spent seven years preventing him from making it in their jersey as well. Graduating to the majors in 1984, the lanky lefty was overshadowed by the jaw-dropping debut of Dwight Gooden, but his stuff was only slightly less electric and he paced the American League in strikeouts each of his first three seasons. He should have been given a team to lead to victory just like the one that was led over him in 1995, but management and ownership whittled away the lineup behind him and eventually shuffled him off to Montreal for his eventual successor in Randy Johnson. Langston did get one last laugh, if a mirthless one: Unlike the M's, he did reach the World Series with the Padres at the age of 37.

ERIK HANSON, RHP (1988-1993)
If there's a surprise on this list for the casual fan, Hanson is probably the one. The only black ink on Hanson's career stat line came in 1992, when he tied for the league lead in losses with 17; that offseason, the M's unceremoniously shipped him off to Cincinnati, the latest casualty of the team's accursed "Young Guns" rotation of Johnson, Hanson, Brian Holman, and Scott Bankhead. Given that one of those four is now ranked among the greatest pitchers in baseball history, it's easy to forget that through 1993 Hanson was clearly the better pitcher, wielding a gorgeous curveball that streaked downward toward the plate like a falling star. He was also the man who pitched the greatest game in Mariners history, a 10-inning, 11-strikeout, 2-hit, 0-run performance. It was, fittingly, also a loss, as the bullpen blew the scoreless game in the eleventh.

RANDY JOHNSON, LHP (1989-1998)

The essence of Randy Johnson's career as a Seattle Mariner isn't in the numbers, though the numbers were great—Randy's 1995 season was as dominant as any this side of Pedro Martinez's 1999—but in his face. Griffey was effortlessly great, Edgar an invincible robot, but it was Randy, his snarling expression and sweat-whipped hair and 100-mph fastball, that stood up to and destroyed almost two decades of defeatist, losing culture. A protege of Nolan Ryan's, Johnson also walked a ridiculous number of batters in his youth, but that actually served as a benefit to his later career. Johnson didn't just throw hard; he wielded a nearly uncontrollable hatred for the batter so great that it struck fear in hitters, distilled in a slider dubbed "Mr. Snappy" that broke like the lunge of a snake. Eventually the team he carried in 1995 grew too heavy for him, and he went on to even greater success (and a World Series championship) in Arizona. One could argue that the former was, given the context of Mariners baseball, the more impressive feat. As one of the greatest pitchers in history and one of the most imposing, he'll be remembered by every town he represented, but it's Seattle that owes him the most.

JAMIE MOYER, LHP (1996-2006)

Jamie Moyer threw slower than a lot of people drive to work in the morning. His age was the most distinctive aspect of his career—the M's traded him to the Phillies in 2006, when he was 43, to give him one more shot at winning the World Series, and he did, two years after that—but the 81-mph fastball is a close second. The best professional athletes are supposed to make it look easy through their effortless athleticism; Moyer made it look easy because he threw as hard as the guy in your dad's men's league, and no one could really understand how he made it work. He had good but hardly pinpoint control, gave up plenty of fly balls, posted low but not FIP-breaking BABIPs (a career .283). It just worked, and it worked for so long that it's impossible to dismiss it as luck. Moyer was the perfect baseball player to root for because everyone just wanted to see it keep working: Because if it did for him, maybe it meant it would work for them, somehow, somewhere.

FREDDY GARCIA, RHP (1999-2004)

One could argue that Garcia was the real end of the line for the Seattle Mariners. The franchise had always traded away its heroes for some reason or another, but the Mark Langston-Randy Johnson-Freddy Garcia trade tree had always kept the team with a headliner at the top of the rotation. The Chief wasn't as overpowering as his predecessors; his strikeout and walk totals were pedestrian. His quiet and precocious efficiency made him the perfect ace for the veteran 2001 club. When the wheels fell off the franchise in 2004, it was Garcia's turn to go, and this time the pipeline broke; he was traded for Miguel Olivo and Jeremy Reed. Garcia spent the rest of his career as a serviceable back-end starter, and the Mariners spent the rest of his career in dire need of one or two just like him.

HISASHI IWAKUMA, RHP (2012-2017)
Few players feel fated to have been a Mariner, and for fewer still does it feel like a compliment. Iwakuma was nearly a catcher in his early years in the NPB, nearly signed with Oakland the year before he joined the M's, and nearly signed a three-year deal with the Dodgers before LA nixed it, citing concerns over medicals. Instead he spent his entire major league career with Seattle, a stalwart right-hand man for Felix Hernandez during Seattle's almost-there Jack Zduriencik era. Like other Japanese pitchers, Iwakuma wielded the two-strike split-finger to full effect, though his was less a strikeout pitch than a homing missile that inevitably found the bottom of the barrel. That balky shoulder that ultimately cost him millions seemed to always be a problem, but Kuma always fought through it and often won the battle.

FELIX HERNANDEZ, RHP (2005-2019)
It's too soon. The image of King Felix standing in front of the remaining crowd after his final start at Safeco Field, soaking in one final ovation, neither he nor they wanting to go home: That image still stains the retinas, and it's the wrong one. It's Griffey napping in the clubhouse, Ichiro misplaying a line drive in left: These memories fade and the highlights stay. Felix will appear in an Orioles jersey in the spring and it will sting and clean like bleach. Then, the end days will fade, the highlights will remain, and King Felix will become young again, the excitement and the energy and the indescribable feeling of promise will return. If the first 17 years of Mariners history were marked by a hundred self-inflicted paper cuts, a hundred antiheroes and fools, the second 17-year drought refines into a single, succinct theme: The inability to deliver Felix Hernandez to a single postseason appearance. The 1-0 losses, the organizational yo-yos, and the innings—so many innings, in this era of constant high-effort pitching—all eventually took their toll. Unlike Griffey, he stayed to let the fans witness it. Being a Mariners fan has never been about winning; if it were, people wouldn't be fans for long. It's been about feeling a fleeting kinship with baseball royalty. In the early days of baseball blogging, amidst the repeated columns of sportswriters in New York and Boston fantasizing about freeing Hernandez from Seattle, the catchphrase was "Felix is ours, and you can't have him." Even if he wears orange next year, it'll always be true. He is ours.

A Taxonomy of 2020 Abnormalities

by Rob Mains

I'm going to start this with a trivia question. Trust me, it's relevant. Don't bother skipping to the end of the article to find the answer, it's not there.

Only five players have appeared in 140 or more games for 16 straight seasons. Who are they?

It's a trivia question starting off an essay, so you know how this works: Whatever you guessed, you're wrong. It's okay. As someone who purchased this book, chances are good that you're an educated baseball fan. But the circumstances behind 2020 force us to abandon, or at least seriously question, some of our favorite patterns and crutches for evaluating the game we love.

We just completed what was undoubtedly the strangest season in MLB history. No fans, geographically limited schedule, universal DH, seven-inning twin bills, runners on second in extra innings, a 16-team postseason, a club playing at a Triple-A stadium. Some of these changes will likely persist (sorry), but we've never had so many tweaks dumped on us all at once, at least not since they figured out how many balls were in a walk.

And the biggest, of course, was the 60-game season. The 19th century was dotted with teams that went bankrupt before the season ended, but the lone season with only 60 scheduled games was 1877. That year there were only six teams, the league rostered a total of 77 players (just 16 more than the 2020 Marlins), and batters called for pitches to be thrown high or low by the pitcher, who was 50 feet away. We can say the 2020 season was easily the shortest ever for recognizable baseball.

As such, it'll stand out. Few abbreviated seasons do. Just about everybody reading this knows the 1994 season ended after Seattle's Randy Johnson struck out Oakland's Ernie Young for the last out of the Mariners-A's game on August 11. The ensuing player strike wiped out the rest of the season and the postseason. Teams played only 112-117 games that year.

And many of you know that a strike in the middle of the 1981 season split the season in two, resulting in the only Division Series until 1995. Teams played only 103-111 games that year, the shortest regular season since 1885.

Those two seasons are memorable. So when we see that nobody drove in 100 runs in 1981, or that Greg Maddux was the only pitcher with 180 or more innings pitched in 1994, we think, "Of course. Strike year."

But we don't remember other short years. You might not recall that the 1994 strike spilled into the next year, chopping 18 games off the 1995 schedule. You might've read that the 1918 season, played during the last pandemic, ended after Labor Day due to the government's World War I "work or fight" order. A strike erased the first week and a half of the 1972 season, but that year's best known as the last time pitchers batted in the American League.

The point is, while we don't remember small changes to the schedule, we remember the big ones. The 1981 mid-season strike. The 1994 season- and Series-ending strike. And, of course, the pandemic-shortened 2020 season. We won't need a reminder why Marcell Ozuna's 18 homers were the fewest to lead the National League in a century. (Literally; Cy Williams led with 15 in 1920.)

Now, about that trivia question. The five players are Hank Aaron, Brooks Robinson, Pete Rose, Ichiro Suzuki, and Johnny Damon. The one nobody gets, of course, is Damon, and a lot of people miss Ichiro, whose last season of 140-plus games came garbed in the red-orange and ocean blue of Miami when he was 42. That's half of what makes it a good question. The other half is the two guys whom many think made the list but didn't. Lou Gehrig? His streak started in the Yankees' 42nd game of the 1925 season and lasted only 13 seasons after that. And everybody assumes Cal Ripken Jr. did it, having played 2,632 straight games over 17 seasons. But one of those 17 seasons was 1994, when the Orioles played only 112 games.

My point? *I just told you* everybody remembers the 1994 strike year, but everybody forgets it fell in the middle of Ripken's streak, separating the first twelve years from the last four. Just because we recall something doesn't mean it's always at the front of our minds.

Nobody is going to forget 2020, and baseball is obviously not the main reason. But there will come a time in the future when you're looking at a player's or a team's record, and there will be baffling numbers there for 2020, and you'll think, "I wonder what happened." (Not to mention the missing line for minor league players.) Just like you forgot that the 1994 strike limited Ripken to 112 games.

Try not to forget it, though. The 2020 season resulted in weird statistical results for several reasons.

There were only 60 games.

I know, duh. But that had impacts beyond counting stats like Ozuna's home run total or Yu Darvish and Shane Bieber leading the majors with eight wins. (I know, pitcher wins, but still.)

The 162-game season is the longest among major North American sports, and that duration gives us a gift. Over the course of a long season, small variations tend to even out. A player who has a ten-game hot streak will probably have a ten-game cold streak. A team that starts the year losing a bunch of close games will probably win a bunch of them. We get regression to the mean. Statistics stabilize.

Consider flipping a coin. Over the long run, we expect it to come up heads about half the time. But the fewer flips, the more variation there'll be. If you flip a coin six times, probability theory tells us you'll get at least two-third heads about 34 percent of the time. Flip it 30 times, your chance of two-thirds heads drops to five percent.

Or, relevant to this case, if you flip a coin 60 times, your chance of getting at least 36 heads—that's 60 percent—is 7.75 percent. Expand the coin-flipping to 162 times, and the chance of getting 60 percent heads drops to 0.73 percent.

In other words, the odds of an outcome that's 20 percent better (or worse) than expected is *more than ten times higher* when you flip your coin 60 times than when you do it 162 times. Call it small sample size, call lack of mean reversion, or call it luck not evening out, 162 is a lot more predictive than 60. You get much more variation over 60 games than over 162. Bieber's 1.63 ERA and 0.87 FIP aren't something we'd see over a full season, and neither is Javier Baéz's .203/.238/.360.

Some players' lines in 2020 look normal. Brian Anderson had an .811 OPS in 2019 and an .810 OPS in 2020. (He probably would have gotten that last point if he'd been given enough time.) But there are many like Bieber and Baéz, some of them from young players still establishing their talent levels. The answer to the question, "What went right or wrong for that guy in 2020?" is most likely "Nothing, it was just a 2020 thing."

Preseason training was abbreviated for hitters.

Every year, spring training drags. Players get tired of it, fans get tired of it, and you sure can tell sportswriters get tired of it. Yes, something to get everyone into shape is necessary, but does it really have to drag on for over a month? Can't we shorten it?

The 2020 season answered in the negative, at least for hitters. Warren Spahn is credited with saying that hitting is timing and pitching is upsetting timing. It appears nobody had his timing down after the abbreviated July summer camp. Through August 9—18 games into the season—MLB batters were hitting .230/.311/.395 with a .275 BABIP. That BABIP, had it held, would have been the lowest since 1968, the Year of the Pitcher. In recent years it's hovered around .300.

It didn't hold. Play returned to more normal levels the rest of the year: .249/.325/.425 with a .297 BABIP starting August 10. But batters whose play concentrated in those first two weeks wound up with ugly lines. Andrew

Benintendi went on the injured list with a season-ending rib cage strain on August 11. His final line: .103/.314/.128 in 14 games. Franchy Cordero went on the IL with a hamate bone fracture on August 9 and a .154/.185/.231 line. Even though he came back strong in a late September return, it was too late to repair his full-season numbers.

Preseason training was abbreviated for pitchers.

Every year, spring training drags. Players get tired of it, fans get tired of it ... wait, I already said that. But the abbreviated preseason was tough on pitchers, too. As noted, they had the upper hand coming out of the gate. But then they lost that hand. And then their arms, too.

The 2020 season was spread over 67 days. During those 67 days, 237 pitchers hit the Injured List, compared to 135 in the first 67 days of 2019. A lot of those IL stints, though, were COVID-19-related. Still, over the first 67 days of the 2019 season, there were 72 pitchers on the IL with arm injuries. That figure jumped to 110 in 2020, a 53 percent increase.

There are a number of factors contributing to pitcher arm injuries, ranging from usage to velocity, but it appears that attenuated preseason training played a role. A lot of pitchers had super-short seasons due to arm woes. Corey Kluber, Roberto Osuna, and Shohei Ohtani combined for seven innings, none after August 8. All suffered arm injuries. We'll never know whether they'd have fared better with a longer preseason, but we can guess how they probably feel.

Everybody played.

Rosters were set to expand from 25 to 26 in 2020, so even if we'd had a normal season, we'd have likely seen 2019's record of 1,410 players on MLB rosters broken. But due to the pandemic, rosters started the year at 30 and were cut to only 28. Add multiple COVID-19 absences and the revolving door caused by poor starts by hitters and a rash of pitcher arm injuries, and 1,289 players appeared in MLB games in 2020. The comparable figure over the first 67 days of the 2019 season was 1,109. That 16 percent increase works out to an average of six more players per team in 2020 compared to a similar slice of 2019. A future look back at 2020 rosters will include a lot of unfamiliar names.

Plus became a minus.

In advanced metrics, we adjust batter and pitcher performance for park and league/era variations. A plus sign appended to the end of a measure means that it's adjusted for park and league. It's scaled to an average of 100, with higher figures above average and lower figures below average. (Similarly, a metric with a minus is also park- and league-adjusted and scaled to 100, with lower values better.) Here at BP, our advanced measure of offensive performance is DRC+. Baseball-Reference has OPS+ and FanGraphs has wRC+.

Using park and league adjustments, we can compare Dante Bichette's 1995 Steroid Era season at pre-humidor Coors Field (.340/.364/.620, 40 homers, 128 RBI, MVP runner-up) with Jim Wynn's 1968 Year of the Pitcher season at the cavernous Astrodome (.269/.376/.474, 26 homers, 67 RBI, no MVP votes). It's not close. DRC+, OPS+, and wRC+ all give the nod to Wynn, handily. This is a useful tool. As my Baseball Prospectus colleague Patrick Dubuque tweeted last fall, "Please note that when I ask how you are, I am already adjusting for era."

The 2020 season messes up plus (and minus) stats for two reasons. First, the park adjustment was based on only 30 home games instead of the usual 81. Everything noted above regarding the short season applies, literally doubly, to park effect calculations. DRC+ uses a single-season park factor. OPS+ uses a three-year average and wRC+ five years. The figure for 2020 is suspect.

Second, OPS+ and wRC+ adjust for league: American and National. (DRC+ adjusts for opponent, regardless of league.) While there were two leagues in 2020, they were an artificial construct. To reduce travel, teams played opponents geographically, not based on league. There weren't two leagues, American and National. There were three, Western, Central, and Eastern.

That makes a difference because teams in the same league played in different run-scoring environments. AL teams scored 4.58 runs per game, NL teams 4.71. That's a small difference. But teams in the East scored 0.21 more runs per game (4.95) than teams in the West (4.74), and they both scored a lot more than Central teams (4.25). Adjusting for league misses that difference, so this book will be safe in that regard, but other sources may be distorted somewhat.

Not every game was a "game."
In 2020, the rising tide of strikeouts was finally stemmed. Strikeouts per team per game fell from 8.8 in 2019 to 8.7 in 2020. That marked the first decline after 14 straight annual increases.

In 2020, the rising tide of strikeouts rose higher. Batters struck out in 23.4 percent of plate appearances compared to 23.0 percent in 2019. That marked the 15th straight annual increase.

Both are true statements.

Because of two rule changes—seven-inning doubleheaders and runners on second in extra innings—games in 2020 were unprecedented in their brevity. There were 37.0 plate appearances per game in 2020. The only years with fewer were 1904 and 1906-1909. The average game in 2020 entailed 8.61 innings pitched, the fewest since 1899.

So when you see any per-game stats for 2020, you need to increase them by 3 or 4 percent to get them on equal footing with recent years.

Or, better, just ignore them. Last year happened. There were major league games contested between major league teams. But when you're looking at those physical or electronic baseball cards, when you're weaving narratives over why this young player's inevitable rise to stardom fell apart or why that old veteran rekindled his magic, don't linger on the 2020 line. It was just too weird.

Thanks to Lucas Apostoleris for research assistance.

—Rob Mains is an author of Baseball Prospectus.

Tranches of WAR

by Russell A. Carleton

We ask "replacement level" to be a lot of things. Sometimes contradictory things. Sometimes I wonder if we know what it even means anymore. The original idea was that it represented the level of production that a team could expect to get from "freely available talent", including bench players, minor leaguers, and waiver wire pickups. It created a common benchmark to compare everyone to, and for that reason, it represented an advancement well beyond what was available at the time. In fact, it created a language and a framework for evaluating players that was not just better but *entirely* different than what came before it.

But then we started mumbling in that language. The idea behind "wins above replacement" was one part sci-fi episode and one part mathematical exercise. Imagine that a player had disappeared before the season and suddenly, in an alternate timeline, his team would have had to replace him. The distance between him and that replacement line was his value. We need to talk about that alternate timeline.

Without getting too into 2:00 am "deep conversations" with extensive navel-gazing, it's worth thinking about why one player might not be playing, while another might.

- A player might not be playing because he has a short-term injury or his manager believes that he needs a day off.
- A player might not be playing because he has a longer-term injury that requires him to be on the injured list.

There's a difference here between these two situations. In particular, the first one generally *doesn't* involve a compensatory roster move, while the second one does. It's possible, though not guaranteed, that the person who will be replacing the injured/resting player would be the same in either case. That matters. Teams generally carry a spare part for all eight position players on the diamond, although in the era of a four-player bench, those spare parts usually are the backup plan for more than one spot.

A couple of years ago, I posed a hypothetical question. Suppose that a team had two players in its system fighting for a fourth outfielder spot. One of them was a league average hitter, but would be worth 20 runs below average if allowed to play center field for a full season. One of them was a perfectly average fielder, but would be 15 runs below average as a hitter, if allowed to play an entire season. Which of the two should the team roster? It's tempting to say the second one, as overall, he is the better player. That misses the point. A league average hitter on the bench isn't just a potential replacement for an injured outfielder. He might also pinch hit for the light-hitting shortstop in a key spot. You keep the average hitter on the roster, even though he isn't a hand-in-glove fit for one specific place on the field, because being a bench player is a different job description than being a long-term fill-in for someone. If you find yourself in need of a longer-term fill-in, you can bring the other guy up from AAA.

When we're determining the value of an everyday player though, if he had disappeared before the season and a team would have had to replace his production, they likely would have done it with a player who was a long-term fill-in type because they would have had to replace a guy who played everyday. Maybe that's the same guy that they would have rostered on their bench anyway, but we don't know. It gets to the query of what we hope to accomplish with WAR. Are we looking for an accurate modeling of reality or are we looking for a common baseline to compare everyone to? Both have their uses, but they are somewhat different questions.

Let's talk about another dichotomy.

- A player might not be playing because he isn't very good and is a bench-level player.
- A player might not be playing because there is another player on the team who has a situational advantage that makes him the better choice today. The classic case of this is a handedness platoon. On another day, he might be a better choice.

When we think about player usage, I think we're still stuck in the model that there are starters and there are scrubs. We have plenty of words for bench players or reserves or backups or utility guys. We do still have the word "platoon" in our collective vocabulary, but in the age of short benches, it's hard to construct one. It's always been hard to construct them. You have to find two players who hit with different hands, have skill sets that complement each other, and probably play the same position. In the era of the short bench, one of them had probably better double as a utility player in some way. Baseball has a two-tiered language geared toward the idea of regulars and reserves. The fact that it was so easy for me to find plenty of synonyms for "a player whose primary function is to come into a game to replace a regular player if he is injured or resting" should tell you something.

I'm always one to look for "unspoken words" in baseball. What is it called when someone is both half of a platoon and the utility infielder? That guy exists sometimes, but he reveals himself in that role—usually by accident. We don't have a word for that, and whenever I find myself saying "we don't have a word for that", I look for new opportunities. What do you call it, further, when the job of being the utility infielder is decentralized across the whole infield with occasional contributions from the left fielder? It's not even a "super-utility" player. What happens when you build your entire roster around the idea that everyone will be expected to be a triple major?

⚾ ⚾ ⚾

I think someone else beat me to this one, and on a grand scale. Platoons work because we know that hitters of the opposite hand to the pitcher get better results than hitters of the same hand, usually to the tune of about 20 points of OBP. If you want to express that in runs, it usually comes out to somewhere around 10 to 12 runs of linear weights value prorated across 650 PA. But hang on a second, now let's say that we have two players who might start today, both of roughly equal merit with the bat. One has a handedness advantage, but is the worse fielder of the two. In that case, as long as his "over the course of a season" projection as a fielder at whatever position you want to slot him into is less than a 10-run drop from the guy he might replace, then he's a better option today.

We're not used to thinking of utility players as bat-first options, who would play below-average defense at three different infield positions. That guy might hook on as a 2B/3B/LF type (Howie Kendrick, come on down!) but teams usually think to themselves that they need as their utility infielder someone who "can handle" shortstop, the toughest of the infield spots to play. If someone can do that *and* hit well, he's probably already starting somewhere, so he's not available as a utility infielder. It's easier for those glove guys to find a job. In a world where the replacement for a shortstop *has to be* the designated utility infielder, that makes sense.

But as we talked about last week, we're living in a different world. The rate at which a replacement for a regular starter turns out to be *another starter* shifting over to cover has gone way up over the last five years. There was always some of it in the game, but this has been a supernova of switcheroos. Now if your second baseman is capable of playing a decent shortstop, that 2B/3B/LF guy can swap in. He's not actually playing shortstop, and maybe the defense suffers from the switch, but if he's got enough of a bat, he might outhit those extra fielding miscues. And in doing so, he is effectively your backup shortstop.

Somewhere along the lines, teams got hip to the idea of multi-positional play from their regulars. I've written before about how you can't just put a player, however athletic, into a new position and expect much at first. The data tell us that. Eventually, players can learn to be multi-positionalists, but it takes time, roughly on the order of two months, before they're OK. But there's a hidden message in there. If you give a player some reps at a new spot, he's a reasonably gifted athlete and somewhat smart and willing to learn, he could probably pick it up enough to get to "good enough," and it doesn't take forever. You just have to be purposeful about it. Maybe you get to the point where you can start to say "he's still below average but we could move him there and get another bat into the lineup, and it's a net win."

Teams have started to build those extra lessons into their player development program. It used to be seen as a mark of weakness to be relegated to "utility player" because that meant that you were a bench player (all those synonyms above come with a side of stigma). Now, it's a way of building a team. If you get a few reps in the minors (where it doesn't count) at a spot, you'll have at least played the spot at game speed before. There are limits to how far you can push that. A slow-footed "he's out in left field because we don't have the DH" guy is never going to play short, but maybe your third baseman can try second base and not look like a total moose out there.

⚾ ⚾ ⚾

Back to WAR. I'd argue that the world of starters and scrubs is slowly disintegrating, for good cause. In the event that a regular starter really does go down with an injury–ostensibly, the alternate universe scenario that WAR is attempting to model–it makes the team a little more resilient to replacing him. And the good news is that you're more likely to be able to replace him with the best of the bench bunch, rather than the third-best guy, because the best guy doesn't have to be an exact positional match for the guy who got hurt. And that's what the manager would want to do. He'd want to replace that long-term production, not with an amalgam of everyone else who played that position, but with the best guy available from his reserves.

Now this is still WAR. We still want to retain the principle that we should be measuring a player, and not his teammates. We need some sort of common baseline, and despite what I just said, we'll still need some sort of amalgam. To construct that, I give to you the idea of the tranche. The word, if you've not heard it before, refers to a piece of a whole that is somehow segmented off. It's often used in finance to talk about layers of a financial instrument.

Here, I want you to consider that there are 30 starters at each of the seven non-battery positions (catchers should have their own WAR, since only a catcher can replace a catcher). We can identify them by playing time, and we can futz around with the definition a little bit if we need to. Next, among those who aren't in that starting pool, we identify the top tranche of the 30 best bench players, which I would again identify by playing time, and then the second and third and fourth and so on. If a player were to disappear, his manager would probably want to take a guy from that top tranche of the bench to replace him. In a world where even the starters can slide around the field, that becomes more feasible.

We can take a look at that top tranche and say "How many of them showed that they are able to play (first, second, etc.)?" and therefore could have directly substituted for the starter? How many of them could have been a direct substitute for our injured player? We don't know whether one of them would be on *a specific* team, but we can say that 40 percent of the time, a manager would have been able to draw from tranche 1 in filling the role, and 35 percent from tranche 2. But on tranche 1, we can also look at how many of those players played a position that could have then shifted and covered for that spot. We'd need some eligibility criteria for all of this (probably a minimum number of games played) but it would just be a matter of multiplication. Shortstop would be harder to fill, and managers would probably be dipping a little further down in the talent pool, and so replacement level would be lower, as it is now.

Doing some quick analysis, I found that the difference in just batting linear weights (haven't even gotten into running or fielding) between tranche 1 and tranche 2 in 2019 was about 6.5 runs, prorated across 650 PA. Between tranche 1 and tranche 3, it's 10.8 runs. The ability to shift those plate appearances up the ladder has some real value.

This part is important. We can also give credit to starters for the positions that they showed an ability to play, even if they didn't play them (this is the guy fully capable of playing center, but who's in a corner because the team already has a good center fielder) because he allows a team to carry a player who hits like a left fielder to functionally be the team's backup center fielder. He facilitates that movement upward among the tranches. We can start to appreciate the difference between a left fielder who would never be able to hack it in center (and the compensatory move that his team would have to make) and the left fielder who could do it, but just didn't have to very often.

Past that, you can continue to use whatever hitting and fielding and running metrics you like to determine a player's value, but when we get down to constructing that baseline, I'd argue we need a better conceptual and mathematical framework. It's going to require some more #GoryMath than we're used to, but I'd argue it's a better conceptualization of the way that MLB actually plays the game in 2020. If…y'know…MLB plays in 2020. If WAR is going to be our flagship statistic among the *acronymati*, then we need to acknowledge that it contains some old and starting-to-be-out-of-date assumptions about the game. We may need to tinker with it. Here's my idea for how.

—*Russell A. Carleton is an author of Baseball Prospectus.*

Secondhand Sport

by Patrick Dubuque

Back before time stopped, I liked to go to thrift stores. Now that I'm older, I rarely ever buy anything—I don't need much in my life, now—but I still enjoy the old familiar circuit: check to see if there are baseball cards to write about, look for board or card games to play with the kids, scan for random ironic jerseys, hit the book section. It takes ten, maybe fifteen minutes. Thrift stores are the antithesis of modern online shopping, because you don't know what they have, and you don't even really know what you want. It's junk, literal junk, stuff other people thought was worthless. That's what makes it great.

In an idealized economy, thrift stores shouldn't exist. Everybody has a living wage, and every product has a durability that exactly matches its desired life; nothing should need to be given away, no one should need to be given to. But then, thrift stores shouldn't work on a customer experience level, either. You wouldn't think an ethos of "let's make everything disorganized and hard to find" would lead to customer satisfaction, but low-budget retailers like TJ Maxx and Ross thrive on this model. People like bargain hunting as much for the hunting as the bargain; it's part of the experience, spending time as if it's a wager. There's a thrill, occasionally, in inefficiency.

In sports, the modern overuse of the word "inefficiency" is a condemnation: It insinuates that there is *an* efficiency, a correct way to be found, and that all other ways are wrong ways. It's prevalent in baseball but hardly contained to it; the lifehack, the Silicon Valley disruption are other examples of productivity creep in our daily lives. Their modern success makes plenty of sense. Maximization of resources, after all, is its own puzzle, and an industry of European board games is founded upon it. It's fun to take a system and optimize it, unravel it like a sudoku puzzle. If there's only one kind of genius, after all, there's no way anyone can fail to appreciate it.

Baseball has been hacking away at these perceived inefficiencies since its inception: platoons, bullpens, farm systems were all installed to extract more out of the tools at hand. But it's been a particular badge of the sabermetric movement, from Ken Phelps and his All-Star Team to Ricardo Rincon and the darlings of *Moneyball*. It's business, but it's also an ethos: the idea that there's treasure among the trash, something we all failed to appreciate until someone brought it to light.

It's the myth that made Sidd Finch so enticing, that fuels so many "best shape" narratives and new pitch promises. We all, athletes and unathletic sportswriters, want to believe that there's genius trapped inside us, and that it's just a matter of puzzling out the combination to unlock it. That our art, our style is the next inefficiency, waiting for our own Billy Beane. It's why we root for underdogs, and why we're excited for the Mike Tauchmans and the Eurubiel Durazos, champions of skin-deep mediocrity.

Except we aren't anymore, really. The days of "Free X" have descended beyond the ring of irony and into obscurity. There are still Xs to be freed, or at least one X, duplicated endlessly: Mike Ford, Luke Voit, Max Muncy. The undervalued one-dimensional slugger demonstrated how the game hasn't quite culturally caught up to its logical extreme. But for those who don't fit the rather spacious mold, times are grimmer. As Rob Arthur revealed several months ago, there's been a marked increase in the number of sub-replacement relievers. It's the outcome of a greater number of teams forced to play out games without the talent to win them, but it's also emblematic of the modern tendency of teams to dispose of their disposable assets, burning through cost-controlled arms the way that man chopped down forests in *The Lorax*. Stuff just isn't built to outlive their original owners anymore.

It's unsurprising, given how well-mined the market for inefficiencies has been of late. The disciples of the early analytics departments, and the disciples of those, have proliferated the league, with only a few backwater holdouts. The league has grown smarter, but every team has learned the same lesson. In fact, the phenomenon creates a peculiar kind of feedback loop: As teams value a specific subset of players or skills, prospective athletes learn to increase their own marketability by conforming themselves to the demands of their prospective employers.

And that's tragic, in the way that the extinction of animals is tragic; a certain amount of biodiversity in baseball has been lost. Shortstops hit like outfielders. Pitchers don't hit at all. Only the catchers remain idiosyncratic, thanks to the defensive demands of their position; eventually they too will be required to produce like everyone else, or they'll meet the fate of their battery mates. A perfect economy requires perfect production.

I mentioned earlier that more and more, I leave thrift stores empty-handed. It is true that I am more discerning than in the past; my bookshelves are full, and there are more streaming films than I will ever be able to watch. But there are other factors at play.

Thrift stores are, in a way, the bond markets of retail. When the economy is rough and other retailers are struggling, more people look secondhand for their products. But as recently as last year, publications were noting a reversal of the trend: Companies like Goodwill and Savers were expanding despite a strong economy. Publications credited a heightened sense of environmentalism and a rejection of cutting-edge fashion as drivers behind the increase, though the more likely answer is the modern American economy hasn't showered its favors equally, particularly among the young.

But it is more than just the economy. Baseball and thrift stores share something else in common, evident in our current conversations about re-starting the sport: They live in the gray area between public service and private enterprise. Thrift stores provide affordable necessities to lower-class citizens, and collectibles and fashion for the middle-class. Because of the success of the latter, prices have gone up across the board. Especially in terms of clothing, the middle-class flight from fashion into vintage has instead carried the aftereffects of fashion, including its costs, into a territory where people just want clothes. But there's another factor in the rise of prices, in the form of the internet.

The Goodwills of the world have grown smarter, too, employing the internet to extract full value from their detritus. Ebay, similarly, has lost much of the charm it had as a new frontier around the turn of the century. Everything has a price point now; even individual taste is no match for the algorithm, because anything rare, no matter how niche its market, is a collectible to someone.

The internet has had the same effect on thrift stores that sabermetrics has had on baseball; its equivalent to OBP was the bar scanner. As detailed in Slate, the rise of second-party stores on eBay and Amazon birthed an entire industry of used-good salespeople, armed with PDAs and scanners, buying books for three dollars to sell online for five. The author, Michael Savitz, reports earning $60,000 by working nearly 80 hours a week; he makes it clear that this is not a vocation of his choosing. It's long hours, with no real creativity or individuality, skimming the cream off of a local establishment and flipping it to someone with a little more money on the other side of the country. And once the vocation exists, the obvious question arises: why wait to put the wares out on the shelves? Why allow value to exist at all?

Nothing is ruined. Thrift stores will continue to sell polo shirts and DVDs, and baseball will continue to exist and make or lose money, depending on who you believe. But as we continue to refine our knowledge, we lose something in the conquest for efficiency, a delight born out of the unknown. The problem isn't the efficiency itself; we can't blame the booksellers, or the people sweeping freeways to collect grams of platinum from damaged catalytic converters. The problem is a system that requires this sort of profit-skimming behavior in order to feed families (or, for corporations, maximize shareholder return).

Seattle Mariners 2021

In times like these, with the 2020 season on the brink and the collective bargaining agreement close behind, it can often feel like the current situation is untenable. It can't keep going like this, even if we don't know what to do about it. But as with thrift stores, there's an equally irresistible feeling that it *has* to keep going, that it would be unimaginable to not have this broken, amazing sport. Both industries exist on an invisible foundation of friction, of chaos and unpredictability, even as both see their foundations buffed down to a perfect, untouchable polish. But if COVID-19 and its financial ramifications do, as some have suggested, make it such that the baseball that returns is fundamentally different than the baseball that came before, perhaps this is the time to lean in, and change the game even more. Fix bunting. Make defense more difficult. Create viable, alternate strategies. Add some chaos back into baseball. It's fun when no one knows quite where things are.

—Patrick Dubuque is an author of Baseball Prospectus.

Steve Dalkowski Dreaming

by Steven Goldman

We dream of being a pitcher, of starring in the major leagues. Depending on your age and your sense of historical perspective, you might imagine yourself as Walter Johnson, throwing harder than anyone else—hitting more batters than anyone else, too, but always feeling bad about it. You could picture yourself as a Tom Seaver or a David Cone, with all the stuff in the world but still being cerebral about it, thinking about so much more than burning 'em in there. There are so many models one could choose: You could be a Lefty Gomez, Jim Bouton, or Bill Lee, skilled, but not taking the whole thing too seriously, or a Lefty Grove, Bob Gibson, or Steve Carlton, powerful but treating each start like a mission to be survived instead of a game to be enjoyed.

Very few would dream of being Steve Dalkowski, the former Baltimore Orioles prospect who died of COVID-19 last week at the age of 80. Yet, there is something just as noble in Dalkowski's negative accomplishments—and accomplishments is what they are—as there is in the precision-engineered pitching of a Greg Maddux. You have to be very good to be that bad. Dalkowski had all of the stuff of the greatest pitchers but none of the command; his story is not one of failing to conquer his limitations, but striving against one of the cruelest hands that fate or genetics or personality can deal us: A desire to achieve great things which is almost but not quite matched by the ability to meet that goal.

As with Johnson, Grove, Bob Feller, and the rest of the hard-throwing pitchers who played before the advent of modern radar guns, we have to take the word of the players and coaches who saw Dalkowski pitch as to his velocity. He was a hard-drinking, maximum-effort pitcher who, if their memories are to be believed, consistently threw over 100 miles per hour. His was the Maltese Fastball, the stuff that dreams are made of. The problem is that velocity without command and control is still a good distance from utility. Dalkowski was the most effective towel you could design for a fish, the sleekest bathing suit intended to be worn by an astronaut, but that doesn't mean he wasn't beautiful: We can appreciate a journey even if it doesn't end at the intended destination.

Whether because of sloppy mechanics he couldn't calm, an inability to understand that a consistent 98 in the strike zone would likely be more effective than a consistent 110 out of it, or all that beer, Dalkowski could never make the adjustments that pitchers like Feller and Nolan Ryan made before him, possibly because he had so far to go: Feller, who never pitched in the minors, came up at 17 and spent three years walking almost seven batters per nine innings before settling in at 3.8 beginning when he was 20. Ryan started out walking over six batters per nine but gradually improved as his long career played out; for him to go from 6.2 walks per nine with the 1966 Greenville Mets to 3.7 with the 1989 Texas Rangers represents a 40 percent reduction. An equivalent improvement by Dalkowski would still have left him walking over 11 batters per nine innings.

Dalkowski was like *The Room* of pitchers, a player so bad he became good again. Cal Ripken, Sr., who both played with and managed Dalkowski, recalled in a 1979 *Sporting News* "where are they now" piece the occasion when the pitcher crossed up his catcher and his fastball, "hit the plate umpire smack in the mask. The mask broke all to pieces and the umpire wound up in the hospital for three days with a concussion. If they ever had a radar gun in those days, I'll bet Dalkowski would have been timed at 110 miles an hour."

Signed by the Orioles out of New Britain High in Connecticut in 1957, Dalkowski was sent to Kingsport in the Appalachian League, where he pitched 62 innings. He allowed only 22 hits in 62 innings, or 3.2 per nine, a number with no equivalent in major league history (though Aroldis Chapman came close in 2014), and also struck out 121 (17.6 per nine) and walked 129 (18.7). He was also charged with 39 wild pitches. That June, one of his fastballs clipped a Dodgers prospect named Bob Beavers and carried away part of his ear. "The first pitch was over the backstop, the second pitch was called a strike, I didn't think it was," Beavers said last year. "The third pitch hit me and knocked me out, so I don't remember much after that. I couldn't get in the sun for a while, and I never did play baseball again." Former minor leaguer Ron Shelton based the *Bull Durham* pitcher Nuke LaLoosh on Dalkowski. And yet, to see him as a figure of fun, an amusing loser, is to misunderstand something unique and strange.

Dalkowski kept on posting some of the strangest lines in baseball history. Pitching for the Stockton Ports of the Class C California League in 1960, he struck out 262 and walked 262 in 170 innings. Yet, he did improve, especially after pitching for Earl Weaver at Elmira in 1962. Weaver had previously had Dalkowski at Aberdeen in 1959, but wasn't ready to grapple with him then. This time he was. "I had grown more and more concerned about players with great physical abilities who could not learn to correct certain basic deficiencies no matter how much you instructed or drilled them," he related in his autobiography, *It's What You Learn After You Know It All That Counts*. He got permission from the Orioles to give all of his players the Stanford-Binet IQ test. "Dalkowski finished in the 1 percentile in his ability to understand facts. Steve, it was said to say, had the ability to do everything but learn." [sic]

IQ tests are problematic diagnostic tools, so take Weaver's estimate of Dalkowski's mental capabilities with a grain of salt. What's important is that even if he got to the right answer by way of the wrong reason, Weaver had learned something valuable. His insight was to stop asking Dalkowski to learn new pitches and just let him get by with the two that he had. Were Dalkowski a prospect today, that would have been a no-brainer: Can't develop a third pitch? The bullpen is right over there, sir. Player development wasn't like that then, but Weaver, temporarily Dalkowski's mentor, could let him work with what he had. According to Weaver, the pitcher responded: "In the final 57 innings he pitched that season Dalkowski gave up 1 earned run, struck out 110 batters, and walked only 11." It's not true—as per the *Elmira Star-Gazette*, as of late July, Dalkowski had walked 71 in 106 innings and finished with 114 in 160 innings, which means Dalkowski's control actually faded at the end of the season rather than improved—but that doesn't mean it didn't happen in some sense, just that it didn't happen that way. Again, it's the journey, not the destination, and his ERA was 3.04 so *something* had gone right.

Also along the way: The next spring, Orioles manager Billy Hitchcock was rooting for Dalkowski to make the team as a long-man—maybe Weaver had gotten through to him. There were things out of Weaver's control, like the universe's twisted sense of humor: that March, Dalkowski's elbow went "twang."

You sometimes read that it was the Orioles' insistence on Dalkowski learning the curve that did him in, but even if they hadn't learned their lesson, the injury was probably just a coincidence: Dalkowski had thrown an incredible number of pitches over the previous few years. Still, it testifies to the dangers of trying to get what you want and risking the loss of what you had. Dalkowski tried to come back, but the 110-mph stuff was gone. A pitcher with no control and no stuff is…a civilian. What followed were years of vagabond living, arrests for drunkenness. There were Alcoholics Anonymous meetings, assistance from baseball alumni associations, but none of it took. From the 1990s until the time of his passing he dwelt in an assisted living facility, suffering from alcohol-related dementia. He'd been a heavy drinker since his teenage years. As with all those pitches per game, there was a price to be paid. You make choices on the journey and some of them are irrevocable. It's like a fairy tale: "Bite of poison apple? Don't mind if I do."

In the aforementioned *Sporting News* profile, Chuck Stevens, the head of the Association of Professional Ballplayers of America, a ballplayer charity, said, "I've got nothing against drinking. I do it myself sometimes. But, I don't condone common drunkenness. We went through lots of heartache and many dollars, but Dalkowski didn't want to help himself and we weren't going to keep him drunk." The journey is *un*like a fairy tale: No one will come along and kiss it better, not if they're busy forming judgments.

In the end, we are left with a sort of philosophical chicken/egg conundrum: Is failing to meet your goals evidence of unfulfilled potential or the lack of it? Isn't what you did by definition what you were capable of doing? Or could you have broken through to something better with the right help, the right lucky break? These are unanswerable questions, and how we try to answer them may say more about us than about the people we're judging.

No pitcher ever has it easy. *All* pitchers must work hard. *All* pitchers must refine their craft. It's almost never just about *stuff*. Dalkowski dreaming is no insult to the great pitchers who made it; from Pete Alexander to Max Scherzer, they have all earned their way up. And yet, if it is true that we can only do as much as we can do, then the journey would be more of an adventure, the ultimate triumph or defeat more noble, if like Dalkowski we lacked 100 percent of the confidence, the command, the self-possession, the commitment, the resistance to making bad decisions that so many great players possess—to be gloriously human. Or, to put it more succinctly, it would be fun to be able to throw as hard as any person ever has. Even if just for a moment, and even if nothing more came of it than that, no one could say you hadn't lived life to the fullest.

—*Steven Goldman is an author of Baseball Prospectus.*

A Reward For A Functioning Society

by Cory Frontin and Craig Goldstein

On July 5, Nationals reliever Sean Doolittle said in the middle of a press conference regarding the restart of Major League Baseball and what would later be known as summer camp, "sports are like the reward of a functioning society." This sentence was amidst a much longer, thoughtful reply about the societal and health conditions under which MLB players were being brought back. It's a very similar sentiment to one Jane McManus used on April 7, when she discussed the White House's meeting with sports commissioners. She said "sports are the effect of a functioning society—not the precursor."

Both versions of the same sentiment spoke to a laudable ideal in the context of a country that was not addressing a rampaging virus, and opting instead to bring sports back for the feeling of normalcy rather than the reality of it. "Priorities," as McManus said.

On Wednesday, the NBA's Milwaukee Bucks conducted a wildcat/political strike, refusing to come out for Game 5 of their playoff series against the Orlando Magic. The Magic refused to accept the forfeit, and shortly thereafter other playoff series were threatened by player strikes. Eventually the league moved to postpone that day's games, folding to players leveraging their united power.

The backdrop against which these actions took place was the shooting by police of Jacob Blake. Blake was shot in the back seven times by police, as he attempted to get into his vehicle. He managed to survive the assault, but is paralyzed from the waist down.

⚾ ⚾ ⚾

The step taken to walk out, first by the Milwaukee Bucks, then subsequently by other NBA, WNBA, and MLB teams, was a step toward upholding the virtue of the sentiment described by McManus and Doolittle. But that sentiment does not align with the broad history of sports in this and other countries, a history that contradicts the core of the idealistic statement.

Sports have been a significant part of American society for most of its existence, expanding in importance and influence in recent years. The idea that society was functioning in a way that was worthy of the reward of sports for most of that time is laughable. Much of America is not functioning and has not functioned for Black people, full stop. The oppressed people at the center of this political act by players, specifically Black players, in concert throughout the NBA and in fits and starts throughout Major League Baseball, have not known a society that functions for them rather than *because* of them.

Politics has been part of the sports landscape since the inception of sport, but for just about as long people have bemoaned its presence. Sports are to be an escape, it is said. An escape from what, though? A functioning society?

No, the presence of sports has never signified a cultural or political system that is on the up and up. Rather, the presence of sports *reflect and reinforce the society that produces them.*

⚾   ⚾   ⚾

The Negro Leagues were born out of societal dysfunction. The need for entirely separate leagues, composed of Black and Latino players barred from the Major Leagues because of racism? That is not a functioning society, and yet there were sports.

Even the integration of players from the Negro Leagues resulted in a transfer of power and wealth from Black-owned businesses and communities and into white ones, mirroring the dysfunction that had bled into every aspect of American society at the time. Japheth Knopp noted in the Spring 2016 Baseball Research Journal:

> *The manner in which integration in baseball—and in American businesses generally—occurred was not the only model which was possible. It was likely not even the best approach available, but rather served the needs of those in already privileged positions who were able to control not only the manner in which desegregation occurred, but the public perception of it as well in order to exploit the situation for financial gain. Indeed, the very word integration may not be the most applicable in this context because what actually transpired was not so much the fair and equitable combination of two subcultures into one equal and more homogenous group, but rather the reluctant allowance—under certain preconditions—for African Americans to be assimilated into white society.*

To understand the value of a movement, though, is not to understand how it is co-opted by ownership, but to know the people it brings together and what they demand. When Jackie Robinson—the player who demarcated the inevitability of the end of the Negro leagues—attended the March on Washington for Jobs and Freedom in 1963, he did so with his family and marched alongside the people. He stood alongside hundreds of thousands to fight for their common civil and labor rights. "The moral arc of the universe is long," many freedom fighters have echoed, "but it bends towards justice." The bend, it is less frequently said, happens when a great mass of people place the moral arc of the universe on their knee and apply force, as Jackie, his family, and thousands of others did that day.

⚾ ⚾ ⚾

Of course, taking the moral arc of the universe down from the mantle and bending it is not without risk. Perhaps the outsized influence of athletes is itself a mark of a dysfunctional society, but, nonetheless, hundreds of athletes woke up on Wednesday morning with the power to bring in millions of dollars in revenues. That very power, as we would come to find out, was matched with the equal and opposite power to *not* bring those revenues. That power, in hands ranging from the Milwaukee Bucks, to Kenny Smith in the *Inside the NBA* Studio, from the unexpected ally, Josh Hader, and his largely white teammates to the notably Black Seattle Mariners, would be exercised for a single demand: the end to state violence against Black people. Not unlike the March itself, it sat at the intersection of the civil rights of Black Americans and bold labor action. The March on Washington stood in the face of a false notion of integration—against an integration of extraction but not one of equality—and proposed something different. Just the same, the acts of solidarity of August 26, 2020 will be remembered in stark defiance of MLB's BLM-branded, but ultimately empty displays on opening weekend.

Bold defiance like this can never be without risk. By choosing to exercise this power, the Milwaukee Bucks took a risk. They risked vitriol and backlash from those they disagreed with. They risked fines or seeing their contracts voided, as a walkout like this is prohibited by their CBA. They risked forfeiting a playoff game, one that, as the No. 1 seed in the playoffs, they'd worked all year to attain. They didn't know how Orlando would respond. It wasn't clear that other teams throughout the league would follow suit in solidarity. And it wasn't known the league would accept these actions and moderately co-opt them by "postponing" games that would have featured no players.

If the league reschedules the games, some of the athletes' risk—their shared sacrifice—will be diminished, in retrospect. But they did not know any of that when they took that risk. And it is often left to athletes to take these risks when others in society won't, especially those of their same socioeconomic status and levels of influence.

It is athletes, specifically BIPOC athletes, that take them, though, because they live with the risk of being something other than white in this country every day. They are no strangers to the realities of police brutality. It seems incongruous then, to say that sports are a reward for a functioning society when we rely on athletes to lead us closer to being a functioning society. Luckily, our beloved athletes, WNBA players first and foremost among them, understand what sports truly are: a pipebender for the moral arc of the universe.

—Craig Goldstein is editor in chief of Baseball Prospectus. Cory Frontin is an author of Baseball Prospectus.

Index of Names

Bishop, Braden 68
Brennan, Brandon 79
Campbell, Isaiah 96
Carlson, Sam 79
Crawford, J.P. 16
Delaplane, Sam 80, 96
DeLoach, Zach 95
Dugger, Robert 34
Dunn, Justin 36
Elías, Roenis 80
Fletcher, Aaron 81
Flexen, Chris 82
Fraley, Jake 69
France, Ty 18
Gerber, Joey 38
Gilbert, Logan 83, 90
Gonzales, Marco 40
Graveman, Kendall 42
Haggerty, Sam 20
Hancock, Emerson 83, 91
Haniger, Mitch 70
Hirano, Yoshihisa 44
Kelenic, Jarred 70, 90
Kikuchi, Yusei 46
Kirby, George 84, 93
Lail, Brady 48
Lewis, Kyle 22
Long Jr., Shed 72
Margevicius, Nick 50
Marmolejos, José 24
Marte, Noelvi 73, 93
Middleton, Keynan 52
Mills, Wyatt 84
Miranda, Aríel 85
Misiewicz, Anthony 54
Montero, Rafael 56
Moore, Dylan 26
Muñoz, Andres 86
Murphy, Tom 74
Newsome, Ljay 58, 97
Phillips, Connor 96
Raleigh, Cal 74, 94
Ramirez, Yohan 60
Rizzo, Joe 75
Rodriguez, Alberto 97
Rodriguez, Julio Y. 76, 89
Sadler, Casey 62
Seager, Kyle 28
Sheffield, Justus 64
Shenton, Austin 97
Steckenrider, Drew 86
Swanson, Erik 66
Then, Juan 87, 94
Torrens, Luis 30
Trammell, Taylor 77, 92
Vest, Will 88
Walton, Donovan 78
White, Evan 32
Williamson, Brandon 96

For the Joy of Keeping Score

THIRTY81 Project is an ongoing graphic design project focused on the ballparks of baseball. Since being established in 2013, scorecards have been a fundemantal part of the effort. Each two-page card is uniquely ballpark-centric — there are 30 variants — and designed with both beginning and veteran scorekeepers in mind. Evolving over the years with suggestions from fans, broadcasters, and official scorers, the sheets are freely available to everyone as printable letter-size PDFs at the project webshop: www.THIRTY81Project.com

Download, Print, Score, Repeat ...

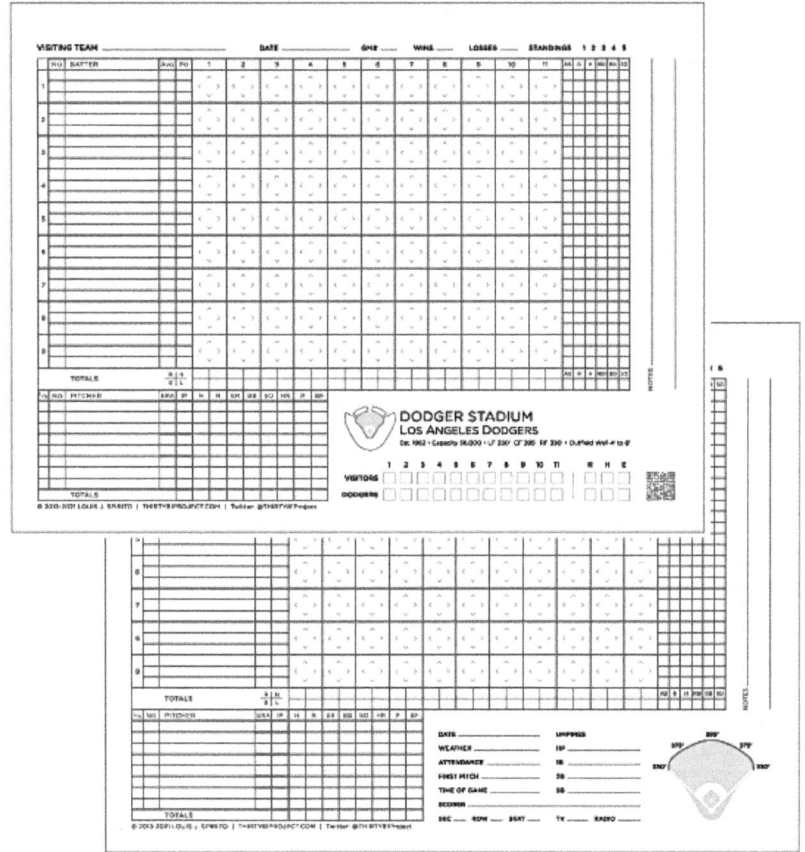